the chrome book

*The Essential Guide to Cloud Computing with Google
Chrome and the Chromebook*

Fourth Edition by **C H Rome** (a pseudonym)

thechromebook.info

Praise for the Third Edition

The Third Edition of this book received the following praise from reviewers on Amazon.com:

"Best Chromebook how-to book and a lot more, too."

"This book is not only a primer, but is clear and complete. BUY IT!"

"Gives you the best instruction for Google and the use of the cloud."

"I could not have started my Samsung Chrome Book without this very helpful guide."

"I recommend this book for all new Chromebook users"

"I would recommend this ebook as a must read before you buy into the Chromebook world.

"This was a good book to get started. I will be going back to it again."

Contents

About the Book

This is the much revised (yet again) and extended fourth edition of "The Chrome Book". I published the first edition in July 2011, which was "early days" in the chromebook story. I published a second edition in November 2012 to coincide with the launch of the very affordable Samsung Chromebook that came armed with an ARM processor. And in March 2013 I published the third edition to coincide with Google's own-brand top-of-the-range Chromebook Pixel. Here I am in July 2013, working on the fourth edition that brings the existing information up-to-date and which adds additional topics in the ever-evolving chromebook story.

While the second edition used the low-cost ARM-powered Samsung Chromebook as the reference model, this edition (like the previous one) uses the top-of-the-range Intel-powered Chromebook Pixel as the reference model. But in many ways it doesn't matter which model I used, or which model you have, because – by and large – all chromebooks operate in exactly the same way, just as all Windows PCs operate in exactly the same way. Regardless of their differing screen sizes, processor speeds, or peripheral ports, what really determines the operation of the chromebook is the version of the Chrome OS operating system that it runs.

So this book is relevant whichever chromebook you are using (or intend to purchase), and I can go further by saying that this book may be relevant even if you're not using a chromebook at all. Since most if not all of the action takes place within the Chrome web browser, some of what you will learn in this book will be relevant to those of you running the Chrome browser on a traditional PC; and particularly relevant to those of you who own both a PC and a chromebook.

It's not all about the hardware and software. It's also about the people, like you and me, who are transitioning (or have transitioned) to the brave new world of cloud computing. While primarily aimed at individual cloud computing converts, I do hint at the possibilities for introducing the Chrome cloud computing model to the corporate enterprise via Google Apps.

As you read through this book you may get the impression that I am some kind of Google evangelist. I suppose I am, but not "religiously" so. A few years ago I may equally have been described as a Microsoft evangelist, and I probably have an old business card lying in a drawer somewhere that says that I once was. The fact is that I am evangelizing Google because right now the Google cloud computing platform comprising Google Apps, the Chrome web browser, and the chromebook computer provides the best all round solution for my personal and business needs. Maybe yours too.

The book is arranged as follows:

In chapter *1 - The Case for Cloud Computing with the Chromebook* I present the case for the new computing paradigm of "cloud computing" in the context of Google's chromebook computers.

In chapter *2 - The Chromebook Computers* I tell you more about the chromebook computers themselves, and what sets them apart from other predominantly Windows-based laptops you may have used in the past.

In chapter *3 - Opening and Operating the Chromebook* I tell you how to interact with your chromebook by using the keyboard, touchpad, and (Chromebook Pixel only) touchscreen to manipulate browser windows, tabs, and other on-screen elements.

In chapter *4 - Web Apps and the Chrome Web Store* I introduce the Chrome Web Store as the source of all the apps you will install on your chromebook.

In chapter *5 - Social Apps* I present some of the apps you might use to interact with other people, predominantly the Gmail and Calendar apps that you may be already familiar with.

In chapter *6 - Google Drive* I demonstrate how Google Drive is used as your "file system in the cloud", and how this can apply to your legacy PC as well as to your chromebook.

In chapter *7 - Google Drive Documents* I present Google's suite of online office apps for creating documents, spreadsheets and presentations.

In chapter *8 – A Quick Look at QuickOffice* I introduce Google's newer Microsoft-compatible alternative office suite that is coming to the chromebook.

In chapter *9 - Google Apps for Your Business* I briefly discuss how chromebooks may be used in a business scenario via the Google Apps variants of the online office programs.

In chapter *10 - Cloud Computing Conundrums* I dig deeper into some of the problems that face ex-PC users who are transitioning to the chromebook. For example: in this brave new world of cloud computing, how do you print or scan documents?

In chapter *11 - Cloud Computing Case Study* I offer a real-life end-to-end scenario for completing a real project (publishing a book like this one) using only web-based apps rather than locally installable programs.

In chapter *12 - Soup Up your Chromebook* with Crouton I present the possibility of installing the "proper" Linux operating system on your chromebook, for those of you who really must use programs like Skype.

In chapter *13 - My (and Your) Head in the Clouds* I conclude by recapping my own progress along the path of cloud computing with Google Chrome and the Cromebook.

I always intended this book to be something of an encyclopedia for chromebook users, hence the somewhat grandiose subtitle "The Essential Guide to Cloud Computing with Google Chrome and the Chromebook". It's taken me a little while to get to this point as the chromebook and Chrome OS has evolved, and as I have built up the content over a number of editions of the book. I now feel that I have come close to achieving my original ambition with this fourth edition; well—as close as it is possible to come in the ever-changing world of information technology.

About the Author

C H Rome is a pseudonym, which I have used because I think it's really clever how it spells out the word "chrome". It's nothing more sinister than that.

1 - The Case for Cloud Computing with the Chromebook

Before we get "hands on" with Chrome and the chromebook in subsequent chapters, I'd like to begin by telling you why I am a believer in the Chrome cloud computing story.

When Google announced on 11 May 2011 that Samsung- and Acer-manufactured chromebook computers running the web-oriented Chrome OS would become available to buy worldwide from 15 June, the question on everyone's lips might have been:

"Why would I want one?"

Some commentators are still asking this question even now that chromebook computers have (finally) achieved a level of sales success and popular acceptance that had eluded Google in the early days.

If you're reading my book because you've just taken delivery of your very own chromebook, you may already have rationalized your decision to own one. Alternatively, you might be thinking "Oh, what have I just bought?" Whether you're thinking about buying a chromebook, or you've already got one, I will help you rationalize the decision you are about to make or have just made.

If you're not in the market for a chromebook right now, you might nonetheless be thinking about moving further towards the more web-centric cloud computing model which no longer obliges you to own a traditional PC or Mac computer. In this case, I will help you rationalize your journey into the cloud, which requires only a web browser (ideally Google Chrome) running on your Linux netbook, Android phone or tablet, Apple Mac, or even your existing PC. In fact, the beauty of Chrome and the associated Google cloud computing ecosystem is that you can begin your cloud computing journey without buying a new device at all. For several months before acquiring a 'proper' chromebook I operated as much as possible in pseudo-cloud mode: interacting only with websites using a combination of my Windows PC and a laptop computer running a pre-release version of the Chromium operating system.

Your Head in the Clouds

How do you spend most of your time on your computer? I bet most of your time is spent shopping online, banking online, booking hotels, emailing, Googling for information, and (for many of you) networking with your friends on Facebook. None of these activities requires a fully functional traditional PC, but all of them depend on your Internet connection. If this is all you do then all you really need is a cheap and cheerful device that acts as the window to your online world. And that's why you need a chromebook.

Okay, so you also write documents and manage spreadsheets which require the full power of the Microsoft Office suite. Or do they? Have you checked out what the free-to-use web-based Google Docs (now Google Drive) office suite can do recently? I know you think that web-based applications are no substitute for 'proper' applications installed on your PC, but didn't you once think that Microsoft Outlook was an irreplaceable PC application for your email, calendar and contacts? If you're like me, nowadays you probably manage all your emails and calendar via a web interface like Google's Gmail or Yahoo! Mail and their associated calendar and contacts web applications.

Welcome to the world of cloud computing, where you *do everything* and *store everything* online. Well, not entirely, as you will see.

Welcome to a world where you no longer need to worry about backing up your important files or keeping your antivirus software up-to-date. It's all done for you. Providing you trust Google, that is.

Welcome to a world where you no longer need to synchronize your mobile phone and PC; a world where – with a complementary Android phone – you can keep your email, calendar, contacts and documents perfectly in sync automatically over the airwaves simply by placing Google at the centre of your online world.

The other major technology companies including Microsoft and Apple also have their own cloud computing strategies and platforms, for example Apple's iCloud service that will make sure everything is synchronized between your various Apple devices. For Apple aficionados this may be a serious cloud computing contender. From my personal perspective, Microsoft would once have been the natural choice for my own venture into the cloud, but I find their Microsoft Office web apps to be too restrictive for my needs because they pretty much necessitate you owning the fully-licensed locally-installed versions of the Office programs anyway—now via their Office365 program. I guess Microsoft has too much investment in PC-based operating systems and office applications to see them die off anytime soon. So for me, at least for now, it's Google all the way.

The Resistance Movement

Despite the apparent advantages of cloud computing in general and of chromebook computers in particular (see next chapter), this new approach to computing is not without its detractors. I put this down to the fact that – believe it or not – no one likes to pay for *efficiency*.

I discovered a while ago that in business people are reluctant to pay for efficiency. If one of my competitors quoted a client $1000 for a job to be completed in four days, and I quoted $750 for the same job to be completed in only two days, guess who the client would choose to do the job?

That's right, not me!

For some deep-rooted psychological reason, some people really are reluctant to pay for efficiency. They don't realize that a job completed sooner at less overall cost (but at an average cost of $375 per day) is better than a job that takes twice as long for more overall cost (but at an apparently lower $250 per day).

Google faced the same problem initially with the chromebook concept. For the price of a chromebook you could buy a reasonably well-specified laptop PC that does everything a chromebook does (i.e. running the Chrome web browser) and so much more besides. Never mind the fact that the chromebook boots up quicker, runs faster, and requires no explicit software updates or virus protection. On the face of it, you were getting "less bang for your buck".

Since I wrote these paragraphs in the early editions of this book, a couple of things have happened:

1. Wintel (i.e. Windows and Intel) powered "ultrabook" laptops came to market, promising the same kinds of boot-up times and sleek appearance as the chromebooks—but with high price tags that made many of the original chromebook models actually look good value in comparison.
2. In October 2012, Samsung launched a significantly less expensive ARM-powered chromebook, which sold well and

which (as a knock-on effect) appeared to have triggered a reduction in the prices of the other chromebook models.

And then Google came full circle, by launching the "reassuringly expensive" Chromebook Pixel with its super-high-resolution touchscreen, speedy Intel i5 processor, and Apple-like minimalist styling. I bought one right away, which I pretty much had to if I'm serious about keeping abreast of new chromebook developments. You might think I was mad to pay the hefty price tag for a computer that ostensibly only runs a web browser, but – as well as being able to use it to "show off" to my friends – I regard it as an investment. I won't need to buy a new chromebook every time Google updates the Chrome operating system, so I can potentially benefit from the large screen, fast processor, and sleek design for many years to come... and, according to the chromebook philosophy, it will be "forever fresh".

A Personal Anecdote

As the neighborhood 'IT expert' I used to be called on regularly to diagnose friends' and families' PC problems... even though my background was in business and systems analysis rather than PC support. To be honest, I hated it. I hated being presented with a plethora of hardware and software compatibility issues when my clients (who were not actually *paying clients*, you understand) were really just looking for a simple way to get online. Sometimes I despaired, and still do, at how personal computers are sold to the general public as though they are consumer items. But consumer items, they are not. When you switch on your TV, you expect it simply to work without having to read the whole manual or attend a 'TV for Beginners' course before tuning into your favorite soap opera. With personal computers it's not so straightforward, as I'm sure you already know. But Google's chromebook initiative might finally be changing that.

Chapter Summary

In this chapter I have addressed such issues as why you would want to adopt the cloud computing model (and buy a chromebook computer) at all. I have highlighted the fact that you probably do most if not all of your "computing" within a web browser, such that the transition to cloud computing is not such a big step

I concluded by explaining why some people were initially hesitant about chromebook computers – because no one likes to pay for efficiency, whether they admit it or not – and I related my personal anecdote about why this new world of cloud computing with Chrome could make my own life easier.

Ready, Steady...

Are you ready to put not just your head in the cloud, but your whole life in the cloud? To have most if not all of your data stored securely (we hope) in a Google data center so that you can access it anytime from anywhere using lightweight and (mostly) low-cost devices such as the chromebook and the desktop-equivalent chromebox? Will you be able to find web-based alternatives to the myriad software programs you have installed locally on your PC?

Let's find out.

Find more **chromebook resources** including **books**, **chromebook computers** (if you don't already have one) and **compatible printers** at usa.thechromebook.info or uk.thechromebook.info.

2 - The Chromebook Computers

This chapter introduces Google's low-maintenance web-centric "chromebook" computers. If you're thinking about purchasing a chromebook, read on. If you've already taken delivery of your chromebook, you can skip ahead to the next chapter, but it still may be worth your while reading this chapter first.

The Advent of Chrome Computing

Google first announced the development of a new lightweight Chrome OS operating system, to be targeted initially at netbook computer users, in July 2009. Two years later the first fruits of those labors came to fruition in the form of the chromebook computers: netbook computers in all but name, which run Chrome OS rather than the traditional Microsoft Windows. Although the first batches of chromebooks looked superficially like laptop computers, they had been designed from the ground up to behave differently and to solve many of the problems associated with the traditional laptop.

In summary, those key features were (and still are):

Always Connected

Unlike a traditional PC where you log into the computer and then separately connect to the Internet, when you log into a chromebook it establishes a Wifi or 3G connection immediately. So you're online straightaway, you stay online, and you don't have to wrestle with network connection settings.

Instant Web

The chromebook boots up from cold start much faster than a traditional PC (in about 10 seconds). But unlike a traditional PC, you will rarely shut it down. Just like when using your mobile phone, you will most likely put your chromebook into standby mode and watch it resume instantly. The optimized Chrome browser loads web pages quickly and (unlike some popular tablet computers) fully supports Adobe Flash web sites.

Same Experience Everywhere

You interact mainly with web sites, not with installed programs. Little or nothing is stored locally on the chromebook computer, and all your documents and settings are stored centrally in 'the cloud'. You don't need to worry about backing up your programs or data, and if you lose your chromebook you can quickly connect to the same online experience using another one.

Friends Let Friends Log In

You can log into your web experience using a friend's chromebook, or they can log into their web experience using yours, and the Chrome browser will automatically reconfigure the settings, apps, and extensions for whoever is logged in. Everything is kept private, and you can optionally allow guests to browse the web without really logging in at all.

Web Apps

Your mobile phone has apps, your tablet device has apps, and your chromebook computer has *web apps* that you can discover in the Chrome Web Store. You don't "install" the majority of these web apps as such; you simply run them straight from the web, and thanks to HTML 5 some of them don't grind to a complete halt if your Internet connection goes down. But in addition to packaged "apps", don't forget the existing web sites you use, which run just as well on the chromebook as ever they did.

Security Built-In

With little or no software installed locally apart from a few optional browser extensions, there is little or no danger from viruses and malware. The security of your operating environment now becomes Google's problem, not yours.

Forever Fresh

You won't be receiving any operating system or software update CDs or DVDs. All of this is done automatically over the air (OTA) behind the scenes; so your chromebook will always be bang up to date and you can carry on computing.

Better Battery Life

If you've been used to getting just 2-4 hours of life out of your laptop between battery charges, you'll be pleasantly surprised by the better battery life that your chromebook provides. But this is dependent on your choice of chromebook model, of course.

Who Needs a Chromebook Computer?

Here are a few of the members of the chromebook target audience (and those who are not):

- Tina is a student living away from home. She likes to socialize via Facebook, to email the folks back home, and to write the occasional essay for her classes. Her university provides free Wifi access to its students. The chromebook is for her.

- Tim wants to get his elderly parents online without the burden of resolving installation conflicts and keeping antivirus software up to date. He merely wants to provide them with a 'window on the web' and a proper keyboard, so the chromebook is for him... or rather, for them.

- Terry is a freelance journalist who researches topics and submits articles to magazine editors, and who otherwise spends his time reading the news and managing his money online. The chromebook is for him.

- Tracey runs a real estate office. Her employees need to take pictures of properties and write descriptions while out in the field, and publish these to the web before even returning to the office. Tracey has a very limited budget for IT support, so a set of team chromebooks backed by the business-oriented Google Apps may be suitable for her and her staff.

- Toby is a trendy 'man about town' who puts style before substance and who likes to show off his cool-brand gadgets to his friends; even though he doesn't use those gadgets to even half their potential. The chromebook was probably not for him... until Google launched the desirable Chromebook Pixel.

- Trisha is a games developer who writes code using a special PC-based software development kit. Her media rich creations necessitate the use of a top-of-the-range video and audio editing software suite. The chromebook is probably not for her... yet!

A Personal Note

When you've been using a chromebook for a little while you'll find yourself loving the almost-instant switch-on, extra-long battery life, and low noise (due to no moving parts) a lot more than you might think. I know I do! If you are lucky enough to use the high-spec Chromebook Pixel, you might surprise yourself with how much you enjoy the hi-res screen experience... not only when watching movies, but also when simply using the web.

This Time It's Different?

This time it's different. Or is it?

In the early days of the chromebook story it certainly looked like things would be quite different. Although chromebooks looked very much like Windows laptops, they didn't operate like them. The only program that could run on your chromebook was the Chrome web browser, and everything you did on the chromebook was via web pages running in the web browser. This was cloud computing in the purest sense.

But something interesting has happened as the Chrome OS operating system has evolved over the past few years—it has started to look more and more like a traditional (think Windows or Mac OS) laptop or desktop operating system, at least from the users' perspective. First a PC-like file explorer was added, with the ability to play media files locally without an Internet connection. Then came a familiar desktop that can display multiple browser windows and which has familiar application bar at the foot of the screen. The more recent has Native Client technology promises to allow applications such as the Google-acquired QuickOffice to run locally on the chromebook itself rather than at the other end of an Internet connection.

In many ways these evolutions have been necessary because (to be frank) many non-technical potential converts from PCs to chromebooks found them to be just "too different" and limiting despite looking superficially identical to traditional laptops on which you could install whatever software programs you liked. In some ways it saddens me slightly that the original "thin client" pure cloud computing ethos has been – for want of a better phrase – watered down, but this is a personal thing.

The Operating System

In any other book about a computer, you would expect to find a chapter or at least a section telling you about the "operating system": the installed system software that basically 'runs' the computer. For PCs, think Microsoft Windows or Linux. For Apple Macs, think MAC OS X. For the Apple iPad, think iOS. And for Android phones, think...Android.

In earlier editions of this book, no such discussion of the operating system was really necessary because *the web browser was the operating system*. That's still largely true, and it's why you can do pretty much the same things (i.e. run the same apps and web sites) on the chromebook as you can on a PC that is running the Chrome web browser. Think no more about whether your computing device runs Windows, Mac OS, iOS, or Linux; think instead about whether it runs Chrome.

So in certain senses, the Chrome web browser is the operating system, but it's rather more subtle that this in two respects:

- The whole point of cloud computing is that most or sometimes all of the processing takes place server-side on the computer that serves up the web pages you use. When you use Gmail or when you order an item from Amazon, your chromebook or PC is acting as something of a dumb terminal—with all of the real "computing" taking place at the other end of your Internet connection.
- The chromebook does have a local operating system, which is a stripped-down version of the Linux operating system, but you'll never really see it unless you perform the steps outlined in chapter *12 - Soup Up your Chromebook with Crouton*. But in recent versions of the Chrome OS (that's the name of the operating system) you will see a familiar PC-like desktop and will

be able to do an increasing amount of computing "locally"; for example playing media files from an attached USB stick.

Chromebook Models

I should say at the outset that all chromebooks should offer essentially the same experience; the differences between them being mainly cosmetic (how nice they look), a matter of performance (how much memory and what speed processor they have), and format (whether they look like traditional laptops or like the alternative chromebox).

The first two chromebooks out of the starting blocks in mid-2011 were the Samsung Series 5 and the Acer AC700. These were followed by the Samsung Series 5 550 and the Samsung "Chromebox"—which resembles a very compact desktop computer, and which you plug into your television screen or dedicated monitor.

In October 2012, Samsung launched (and Google promoted) a new less-expensive chromebook, which helped address previous criticisms that you could do everything that a chromebook can do – and more – using a less expensive traditional laptop. Those criticisms missed the point of the chromebook concept, but they did make people think twice about shelling out what looked like more money for less functionality. It was the less expensive chromebook model that I used as the demonstration vehicle in the second edition of this book; but it shouldn't really have mattered which chromebook *you were using*… or intended to use.

In February / March 2013 Google swung entirely the other way by launching a new top-of-the-range Chromebook Pixel boasting a super high resolution touch screen, super-fast processor, and Apple-like minimalistic styling. The Chromebook Pixel was used as the vehicle for this third edition and this fourth edition of "The Chrome Book". If you're wondering about whether the Chromebook Pixel is really worth the higher asking price, here is my one-sentence assessment: it looks great when closed, almost as impressive when opened, and the screen + sound are truly awesome! If that's not enticing enough, consider this:

The Chromebook Pixel: So Good, I Kept It!

When I ordered my Chromebook Pixel from the Google Play store on the day of launch, I noted that the Ts and Cs of my order allowed a grace period of 15 days within which I could return the device if I didn't like it. Just enough time to add a few paragraphs in *this book* about the Chromebook Pixel unique features such as the touch screen, and then get my money back... minus a possible "restocking fee". But, you know what? The more I used it, the more I loved it, and I found it to be...

So good, I kept it!

This is the most ringing endorsement I can possibly give for the Chromebook Pixel, but do keep in mind that *this book* is relevant to you whichever chromebook model you're using (or intend to use).

During 2013, other manufacturers such as HP have launched their own chromebook models.

Thanks for the Memory

One thing you'll notice about the chromebook specifications is that many of these computers come with so little "hard disk space"; for example on 32GB of SSD storage on the Wifi Chromebook Pixel model. The rationale is that many or all of your apps will run server-side "in the cloud", and most if not all of your data should be stored there too, so there really is no need for a large hard disk. Some local storage is necessary, of course, and in this respect at least the lightweight Chrome OS operating system doesn't eat up as much of the original on-board memory as does (for example) Windows 8 running on a Microsoft Surface Pro.

For those of you who still crave a three hundred gigabyte traditional "hard disk" on which to store all your files, you'll find some chromebook models with those too.

The Chromebox

In the first half of 2012, Google released the "chromebox" desktop equivalent of the "chromebook" netbook or laptop. Attach this compact unit to your TV screen or dedicated display unit, attach a proper keyboard and mouse to it, and you have a relatively inexpensive and efficient way to browse the web and work in the cloud.

The case for the chromebox may be at least as great as the case for the chromebook, because both of them need an almost-permanent Internet connection, and your desktop-replacement chromebox will almost certainly always be within range of a Wifi signal in your home or at work. Having said this, the desktop-replacement chromebox is also so portable that it is possible to pick it up and carry it around, and plug it into someone else's screen wherever you go.

What You Have Been Waiting For

Now that you are armed with some of the background information on cloud computing and the chromebook computers, it's time to move on to something a little more practical... which, do doubt, is what you've been waiting for. Whichever chromebook model you have, it's now time to open the box (if it's new) and operate the chromebook (whether recently arrived or not).

Find more **chromebook resources** including **books**, **chromebook computers** (if you don't already have one) and **compatible printers** at usa.thechromebook.info or uk.thechromebook.info.

---

3 - Opening and Operating the Chromebook

In this chapter you open the chromebook box (if you just took delivery) to see what's inside, and then you learn to operate the chromebook– which may be different from, but in some ways much easier to operate than, the other laptop computers you may have used in the past.

What's in the Box?

It may differ depending on which model chromebook or chromebox you buy, and when you buy it, but the box for the October 2012 edition Samsung Chromebook and the February 2013 edition Chromebook Pixel contained just two items: the computer and a power supply.

There were no installation CDs or DVDs, because they're simply not needed. The whole point is that you're not allowed to install your own software apart from Chrome web apps and browser extensions; and the Chrome OS itself will be updated automatically over the Internet at periodic intervals. It is in this way that the chromebook is designed to remain low-maintenance and virus-free.

To be fair, the box will likely also contain a few flimsy booklets but no comprehensive "manual"—which seems to be the case with most computers these days. The idea is for you to access the chromebook's own built-in and on-line help... and to get extra assistance from books like the one you're reading now.

Accessing the built-in Chrome OS help is as easy as opening the pop-up menu from the status area (bottom-right of screen) like this:

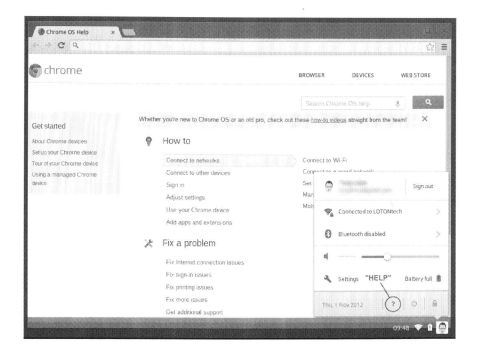

But we're getting ahead of ourselves, because you haven't set up your chromebook yet.

The Chromebook Initial Setup

When setting up your chromebook for the first time, the first thing you need to do is...

Get Connected

The first time you fire up your chromebook – merely by opening the lid – you will be presented with a dialog asking you to **Select your language**, **Select your keyboard**, and **Select a network**. The chromebook is designed to be "always connected" so it makes sense to select a network before you do anything else.

The list of networks you are presented with will depend on whether you have a Wifi-only or Wifi+3G (or 4G) chromebook. I'm running a Wifi chromebook for demonstration purposes, so I am presented with the following Wifi networks from which to choose:

- **LOTONtech** (the name of my company Wifi network)
- **BTFON** (the public network presented by my British Telecom router)
- **OliWifi** (which I assume to be my neighbor's Wifi network)

Actually, I am presented with an additional network named **Ethernet**. This is because I attached my Android phone to the chromebook via a USB cable and enabled the USB Tethering option on the phone. It means I can connect my chromebook to the Internet via the Android phone's 3G signal. You will discover how to do this in chapter *10 - Cloud Computing Conundrums*.

Check for Updates

Once your chromebook is connected to a network, you will likely find that it checks for and installs updates. The idea is that the chromebook is automatically kept always up-to-date with the latest Chrome OS operating system, without you having to manually download and install updates or purchase operating system installation CDs or DVDs.

One thing to keep in mind is that the client portion of the Chrome OS, the portion installed on your chromebook itself, is in any case intended to be small and light, consisting of the Chrome web browser and not much else. The majority of the "apps" you will run will be in the form of repackaged web sites where most of the processing takes place at the other end of your Internet connection.

Sign In

Once connected to a network, you will be asked to **Sign in** to your Google Account if you have one, or to **Create a Google Account** if you don't. You will already have a Google account if you have used Gmail, Blogger or another Google service.

Note that you can sign in to any chromebook using your Google account, and you don't need to worry about the chromebook's owner accessing any of your stuff once you've signed out.

You also have a third option to not sign in at all, and to **Browse as a Guest**. This option is useful if you or a friend simply want to browse the web without associating your activity with a particular Google Account. Note, though, that settings won't be saved when you browse as a guest, and each time will be an entirely new experience. So if you browse as a guest the first time after entering your Wifi network password or key, don't be surprised if you're asked for that same network password or key the next time you log in.

The first time you log in using a Google account, you will be prompted to choose a picture to appear for your account on the chromebook sign-in screen. You can choose one of the default pictures, or your Google+ profile picture, or a picture of yourself staring into the chromebook's webcam.

Whenever you power up the chromebook in future – and assuming other family members, friends or work colleagues have used your chromebook (which is all part of the plan) – then you will be presented with a sign-in screen that allows you to choose which identity (i.e. Google account holder) to log in as; or to **+ Add user** for one of those friends, family, or colleagues.

I'll say more about your Google account later.

Interacting with the Chromebook

You will interact with your chromebook using the keyboard and touchpad, and by manipulating items on the screen. Here's how...

Power On / Power Off

Think of your chromebook as more like your mobile phone, which goes from powered-on to standby (and back again) pretty much instantaneously. Just close the chromebook lid to switch off the screen and go into standby mode, and then flip it open again to resume working immediately.

Note that by default the chromebook will resume without requiring a password, which means that anyone could use it simply by lifting the lid. For greater security you can change one of the User settings, as shown below, to "**Require password to wake from sleep**".

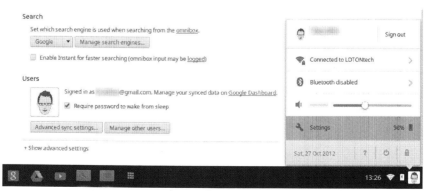

You can also lock your user account at any time without closing the lid, so that a password is required to resume, by pressing the **Power** button at the top-right of the keyboard for one second. Pressing the power button for a few seconds shuts down the chromebook completely, and you can power it up again either by pressing the power button once more or by lifting the lid (if you had closed it).

The Chromebook Keyboard

As you can see below, the chromebook keyboard is a regular QWERTY keyboard with the PC "function keys" (F1-F12) on the top row replaced by some dedicated chromebook keys.

The second and third left and right arrow keys act as shortcut keys for the Chrome browser's *forward* and *back* functions, and the fourth key acts as a shortcut for the browser's *refresh* (or reload) function.

The fifth key acts as a shortcut key for maximizing (making full-screen) whichever browser window you are working in; and the sixth key allows you to switch between browser windows when you have more than one of them open – and it's particularly useful when they are all maximized.

You should see a spyglass key at the left of the keyboard's middle row, in the place where you would expect to find the Caps Lock key. This key is used to initiate a search, but many chromebook users prefer to revert to the traditional use of this key as the Caps Lock key. You can do this via the Chrome **Settings** web page at **chrome://settings/keyboard-overlay** as shown below.

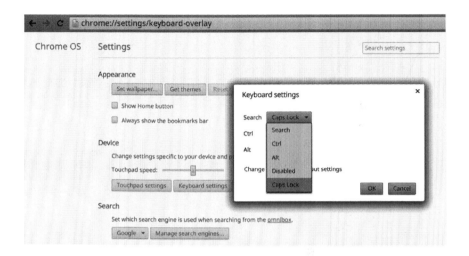

Note that in addition to the dedicated function keys, there are also some key combinations that perform specific tasks, as detailed below. If you don't understand what some of these descriptions mean, just read through the rest of this chapter or the whole book, and then come back here to take another look.

- Pressing the **ctrl** and **t** keys together (**ctrl + t**) opens a new browser tab.
- Pressing the **ctrl** and **n** keys together (**ctrl + n**) opens a new browser window.
- Pressing the **ctrl** and **p** keys together (**ctrl + p**) launches the Google Cloud Print dialog.
- Pressing the **ctrl** and **switch window** key (sixth key on the top row in my picture) together captures a screenshot of what is currently displayed on the chromebook screen, and saves it as a Portable Network Graphics (.png) image in your Downloads

folder. Pressing the **shift** key at the same time allows you to select a part of the screen to be captured.

- Pressing the **ctrl** and **k** keys together (**ctrl** + **k**) invites you to perform a Google Search.
- Pressing the **ctrl** and **j** keys together (**ctrl** + **j**) presents you with the contents of your Chrome browser downloads folder which can also be accessed by typing **chrome://downloads/#** into the browser omnibox (web address bar).
- Pressing the **ctrl** and **h** keys together (**ctrl** + **h**) presents you with the contents of your Chrome browser history which can also be accessed by typing **chrome://history** into the browser omnibox.
- Pressing the **ctrl** and **f** keys together (**ctrl** + **f**) allows you to find (and highlight) specific text on the web page you are viewing.
- Pressing the **ctrl** and **d** keys together (**ctrl** + **d**) adds the current web page to your list of bookmarked web pages.
- Pressing the **ctrl** and **s** keys together (**ctrl** + **s**) opens a dialog that allows you to save the current file; e.g. the web page you are viewing.
- Pressing the **ctrl** and **a** keys together (**ctrl** + **a**) highlights the entire contents on display, which can then be copied by pressing **ctrl** + **c** and pasted into another app by pressing **ctrl** + **v**.
- Pressing the **ctrl** and **o** keys together (**ctrl** + **o**) allows you to **Select a file to open**.
- Pressing the **ctrl** and **u** keys together (**ctrl** + **u**) allows you to view the HTML source code for the current web page. If you don't know what this means, don't worry about it.
- Pressing the **ctrl** and **w** keys together (**ctrl** + **w**) closes the current browser tab.

Note that some of these key combinations only take effect if you have a browser window open.

Chromebook Touchpad

You can plug a USB mouse into one of the USB sockets of your chromebook, and in the case of a chromebox you will have to do so, but the chromebook also has a touchpad at the front of the keyboard which allows you to move the mouse cursor around the screen.

Gliding your finger around the pad moves the mouse cursor, and lightly tapping the pad (or pressing for a more responsive 'click') is equivalent to making a selection by clicking the left mouse button on a traditional mouse. A right-button click – which usually displays a context menu of additional options – is performed by tapping or pressing on the touchpad with two fingers. You can also place two fingers side-by-side on the touchpad and slide them up and down to scroll the screen contents up and down.

The Chromebook Pixel Touch Screen

The Chromebook Pixel is (or was, depending when you read this) the first chromebook computer to feature a touchscreen. It may seem a little gimmicky because browser windows and their contents are not really optimized for touch screen operation, but it is quite intuitive to scroll up and down a lengthy document by swiping your finger up and down the screen. This is one of several "gestures" that you can perform using your finger on the touch screen, the others being:

- **Tap** to *click*
- **Double Tap** to *double click*
- **Long Press** for a *context click* (like a right-click)
- **Scroll** (press and move your finger) to *scroll* or to *drag and drop*
- **Flick** (tap and move your finger quickly) to *scroll fast* or *switch pages*

Another gesture, which will be familiar to users of tablet computers such as the Microsoft Surface, is the ability to **Flick** up from just off the bottom of the screen to reveal the *launcher* bar.

A note about "Pinch and Zoom" on the Chromebook Pixel
Users of other touchscreen tablets, laptops and smartphones will be familiar with another touch gesture – pinch and zoom – which allows you to move two fingers together or apart on the screen in order to shrink or grow (contract or expand, zoom in or zoom out) the content shown on the screen.

You may find that the "pinch and zoom" gesture works in some web apps, such as Google Maps, but not in all apps. Help is at hand in the form of the Chrome experimental flags that you can access by typing the text **chrome://flags/#enable-pinch** into the Chrome browser omnibox (web address bar). Click **Enable**, restart your Chromebook Pixel, and – Hey Presto! – you should now be able to "pinch and zoom" on most if not all web sites and web apps.

Now that you know how to interact with your chromebook using the keyboard, touchpad or touchscreen, you need to know what kind of screen elements you can actually interact with.

The Desktop, Windows, Tabs and Apps

In early versions of the Chrome OS, the screen would show a full-screen web browser… and that was all. The Chrome OS user interface has now evolved to resemble a PC desktop-style display; albeit one that can only really display different browser windows:

The screenshot above shows the distinction between **WINDOWS** and **TABS**. Theoretically you could run separate web apps and display separate web pages using multiple tabs within a single browser window, but I find it useful to have 'batches' of tabs running in different browser windows. For example: I might use multiple tabs within one browser window for my Google email and calendar, and use multiple tabs within another browser window for the online newspaper pages I'm reading. When running these browser windows maximized (click the square icons at the top-right of the windows) you can easily switch between browser windows by pressing the *switch windows* key.

Across the bottom of the Chrome desktop you will find a horizontal *launcher* bar to which you can 'pin' your favorite web apps, and you can see the full list of your apps by selecting the checkerboard icon. This may be reminiscent of the user interface on your Android smartphone, or you can think of it as like the Windows 7 Start Menu.

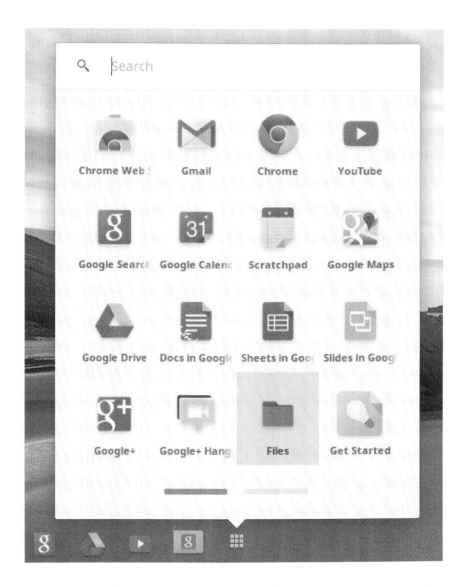

Remember I said that you could pin your favorite apps to the launcher bar? Just right-click – or two-finger touch on the touchpad, or long press on the touchscreen – to display a context menu from which you can select the option to **Pin to Launcher**.

Some of the available apps are merely existing web sites that are accessible via these 'app' shortcuts; and that's the whole point about the Chrome OS– to access most if not all apps via the Chrome web browser when connected to the Internet.

Some of the available apps are locally-installed 'offline' apps that will operate even in the absence of an Internet connection. In the previous screenshot I have highlighted the **Files** app for special attention.

The File Manager

You can launch the Chrome OS file manager by selecting the **Files** app icon as shown above. In this file manager window you will see the available data drives or file storage locations listed in the left-hand column, which will typically include your **Downloads** folder (where documents will be placed when downloaded from the World Wide Web), your **Google Drive** (which is the online storage linked to your Google account), and any external drives such as a USB stick or SD card that you have inserted into one of the chromebook or chromebox USB sockets.

In the following screenshot I have launched a file manager window to view the contents of one of my **Google Drive** folders as thumbnails (note the **View** item in the pull-down menu).

You can move files from one location to another, for example from your USB drive or SD card to your Google Drive... and vice versa. In this case you might right-click (or two-finger tap) the required file to launch its context menu and choose the **Copy** option, and then browse to a folder in the other location before right-clicking again and choosing the **Paste** option to deposit the file at its destination.

The context menu for any given file also allows you to perform some default action on the file—such as **View** (for a PDF), **Open** (for a Google document), or launch the **Chrome Office Viewer** (for a Microsoft Office file such as a Word or Excel file). For Microsoft Office documents, also see chapter *8 – A Quick Look at QuickOffice*.

A note about the Downloads folder

You'll use the **Downloads** folder a lot as a staging post between web apps. For example:

- If ever you take a screenshot of the chromebook screen by pressing the **ctrl + *switch windows*** key combination, the screen image will be placed in your **Downloads** folder, from where you can subsequently select the image when inserting into a Google Docs document.
- In my later case study chapter, I will download both a Google Document and a Google Drawing to my **Downloads** folder, from where I will upload those files to the CreateSpace and Kindle Direct Publishing (KDP) publishing platforms.

In other words, when working on the same artifacts (like images) via a number of web apps, you will very often find yourself transferring them to and fro via your **Downloads** folder.

Opening Media Files

The chromebook has a basic multimedia player that allows you to play songs and movies from the file manager, whether these are on an inserted USB stick or SD card or have been downloaded to your Downloads folder. You don't need to be connected to the Internet in order to play these media files.

There is also a basic image editor that allows you to perform simple functions like cropping an image, changing its brightness, or rotating left or right. To edit an image, just open it via the file manager and click the pencil (**Edit**) icon at the bottom-right of the screen.

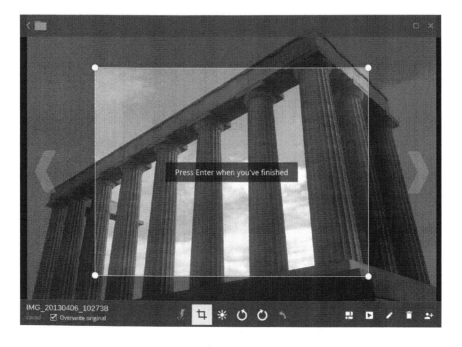

Before you edit an image in any way, note the checkbox at the bottom-left that is checked by default to **Overwrite original** image. If you want the original image to remain unchanged, you *must* uncheck this box before cropping, brightening or rotating!

If your image editing requirements extend beyond what this app can do, you might like to take a look at the Pixlr web app that is available in the Chrome Web Store. If you have installed this app, you will be able to send an image file directly to Pixlr from the file manager by right clicking the file name and choosing the **Open with...** option followed by **Pixlr**.

The Chrome Web Browser

The main app that you will run on your chromebook, and the app which in fact underpins all other apps, is the Chrome web browser which you can access via the app shortcut labeled **Google Chrome** or simply **Chrome**. It has a multicolored circular icon.

Since the Chrome web browser preceded the Chrome OS and chromebook computer by several years, there are already many good books that will tell you in detail how this web browser works. You may already have read one of these books, or maybe you've already used the Chrome browser on your 'legacy' PC. Failing this, you will most likely have used one of the other browsers like Internet Explorer or Mozilla Firefox that do essentially the same job. What is important here, therefore, is to present some of the features of the Chrome browser that distinguish it from other web browsers, particularly when it is running on a chromebook computer.

Tabs and Windows

You are probably already familiar with the fact that the Chrome browser (just like most other web browsers) allows you to open separate web pages in separate browser tabs, and I told you so earlier in this book. The ability to open web pages in separate tabs within a single browser window was a great advance when first introduced to PC web browsers, because it saved you from launching the web browser program multiple times. Nevertheless, it is sometimes useful to have entirely separate browser sessions running, with different arrangements of tabs in each one, so that (for example) you can open all your email message tabs in one window and all your document tabs in another window. For this reason, the Chrome OS allows you to launch separate browser windows and switch between them using the dedicated keyboard key (shown again below) on your chromebook. Pressing it multiple times will cycle through your various browser windows.

Bringing the two ideas of separate tabs and separate windows together, you will be interested to know that you can "tear off" a browser tab to become a separate browser window. In the following screenshot I am in the process of tearing the **Google Drive** tab from my **Google Calendar** browser window so that it becomes a browser window in its own right. And I'm doing so on a regular PC rather than on a chromebook, to illustrate the fact that the Chrome browser operates in pretty much the same way regardless of what kind of computer you are using.

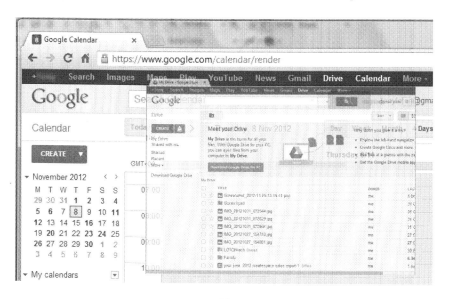

Bookmarks

In the **Customize and Control** menu that you can access by clicking the icon at the top-right of the Chrome browser (see below) you will see a menu option titled **Bookmark manager**, and in the Tools sub-menu you will see an option to **Always show bookmarks bar**.

Just as in any web browser, you can bookmark your favorite web pages so that you can launch them at the click of a mouse... or tap of the touchpad. You can add a bookmark for the web page you are currently viewing by clicking the star icon to the right of the browser address bar.

Where it gets really interesting with the Chrome web browser is when you are signed in to your chromebook or when you "sign in" to the Chrome web browser itself (which is not the same thing as simply signing into your Google Account) on your PC as shown below.

Your bookmarks and browsing history will now follow you to any device on which you sign into Chrome.

Settings

You can access your Chrome browser settings either by selecting **Settings** from the pull-down menu as shown below, or by typing **chrome://chrome/settings** into the browser address bar, or (on a chromebook) by clicking your user picture at the bottom-right of the screen and selecting **Settings**.

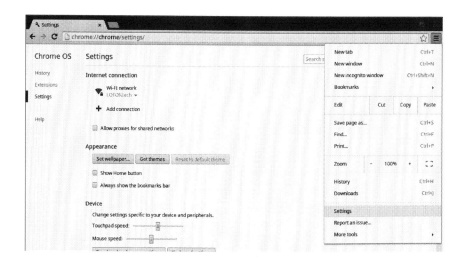

The settings that you can view and configure will depend on whether you're running the Chrome browser on a PC or on a chromebook / chromebox. On a chromebook these settings refer to your settings on the actual device, so in this case they will include such things as **Internet connection** and **Touchpad speed**.

Some of the more interesting settings can be found by clicking the **Show advanced settings** link at the foot of the settings page. For example, the settings for the Google Cloud Print facility that I will explain in chapter *10 - Cloud Computing Conundrums*. When running the Chrome web browser on a chromebook you will find a **Factory Reset** or **Powerwash** option, which may be useful when you decide to sell on your chromebook (why would you?). Otherwise, be careful with this option; but with all of your data stored on the cloud you should be relatively protected if your finger strays towards this "self-destruct" button!

Is the Web Browser Really the Operating System?

At the time of the first iterations of the chromebook concept it could be argued that the web browser was the computer's operating system, because all user activity took place within the web browser.

In more recent iterations, Google seems to have lost its nerve somewhat with the "everything within the browser" paradigm and has introduced a more PC-like desktop. Nonetheless, the Chrome web browser is very much the centerpiece for the chromebook user experience—even for locally installable "offline" apps.

If we ignore the fact that the chromebook client operating system is actually based on Linux (which is largely invisible to the end user, but see chapter *12 - Soup Up your Chromebook with Crouton*), we find that standardization of the user experience within the browser has allowed Google to extend the Chrome OS experience across traditional PCs and other devices in addition to dedicated chromebook and chromebox devices.

This is only half the story as far as the computer operating system is concerned. The fact is that computer operating systems have essentially two parts: the *interaction part* and the *execution part*:

- The *interaction part* of the operating system comprises what you see on the screen (traditionally the Windows desktop) and how you interact with the computer using a keyboard, mouse, webcam, touchscreen, or some externally-connected peripheral such as a scanner.

- The *execution part* is the part of the operating system that allows you to install programs and keep them running.

Whereas the Chrome web browser and the underlying lightweight Linux-based Chrome OS operating system present you with the *interaction part* of the operating system, the *execution part* of the operating system is not necessarily running on your computer at all. This is the world of cloud computing, where when you edit a Google Docs document most of the heavy lifting – i.e. 'running the program' – takes place on Google's own remote server computers.

The computer in front of you may be simply taking your input via keyboard and touchpad, instructing the Google server to crunch your numbers, and then presenting your results in the browser window. It's just like in the old days of mainframe computers and green screen terminals... but now with more colors.

Even computer games are going this way, with an ever-increasing number of games being "streamed" over the Internet to what are (or could be) much-simplified devices.

Your Google Account

When you first set up your chromebook, you had to sign in to an existing Google account or create a new one. You can also "sign in" to the Chrome web browser on your Windows PC or other device, so that certain elements of your experience are shared across devices.

For example, on my chromebook I created a set of bookmarks in a folder named **movies to watch**, and I installed some apps from the Chrome Web Store (see chapter *4 - Web Apps and the Chrome Web Store*). Upon launching the Chrome web browser on my PC, I am presented with exactly the same bookmarks and choice of apps as shown here:

It's your central Google account that makes this cross-device synchronization possible, and it's your Google account that allows you to use Google Cloud Print and the Chrome Remote Desktop. See chapter *10 - Cloud Computing Conundrums* for more details about these facilities.

Your Google account is also the common thread that runs through your Gmail, Google Drive, Blogger (if you use it) and other Google services. I'll tell you more about these shortly.

You can manage your Google account by visiting the web page at https://www.google.com/accounts/ManageAccount or by choosing the **Account settings** link from the pull-down menu of options available when you click the Gmail email address shown at the top-right of your browser pages when using any Google application.

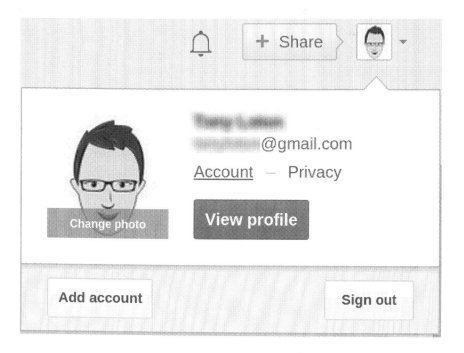

There are various things you can manage on an account, depending on whether it is a personal account or a company (staff) account set up for you by an organization via Google Apps. Two of the most important things you will want to manage are your security and your cloud storage.

Security

The most important thing you will do in your Google Account is to manage your password. Since your Gmail address and password combination is the key to everything stored in your Google cloud, it is important that you remember it while at the same time not making it obvious and guessable.

Fortunately, you are provided with a couple of mechanisms for recovering your password in the event that you forget what it is. You can record an alternative **recovery email address** to which a password reminder can be sent, and you can specify a security question such as "What is the name of your best friend from childhood?" that you will be asked in the event that you wish to reset your password.

Note that if ever you change your Google password – which perhaps you should do periodically – you will have to update any client devices that sign into your Google account. For example, the Gmail application on your Android mobile phone will prompt you for your password when it finds that a connection cannot be made using your old password.

Cloud Storage

At the time of writing, Google provides a limited amount of cloud storage to new account holders who haven't bought a device.

If you bought one of the October 2012 Samsung Chromebooks it is likely that you were offered 100GB of online storage for two years when you first accessed the Files app on the device. At the time, it was worth $5-per-month, therefore $120 in total. Not bad, but do keep in mind that if you fill most or all of the storage during the two years then you will have to commit to the prevailing rate for that level of storage once the offer period has ended. Don't worry, you won't lose any of your files, but you won't be able to store new files on the cloud once the offer period has concluded unless you sign up for a storage plan.

If you bought a Chromebook Pixel at launch towards the end of February 2013 you should have been offered 1TB of cloud storage for up to three years... although in my case this seemed inexplicably to be a two-year offer. Some commentators regarded the free storage in itself to be worth the (high) cost of the Chromebook Pixel. If you were going to purchase 1TB of cloud storage from Google anyway, then you could effectively get the Chromebook Pixel device for free... in a manner of speaking. But the same rule applies as before: at the end of the free period you will henceforth have to pay up or shut up, but you won't lose the files you have already stored.

Google Wallet

Whenever you make purchases of movies, books or music from Google Play, you will do so via the Google Wallet associated with your Google account. This is a "virtual wallet" that stores details of your credit and debit cards and which allows you to pay for purchases from Google and other web sites and stores from your computer or Android mobile phone.

The following picture shows a typical list of transactions that were conducted via the Google Wallet.

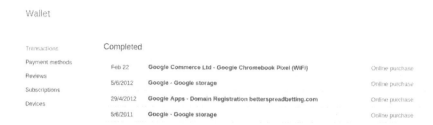

Completed			
Feb 22	Google Commerce Ltd - Google Chromebook Pixel (WiFi)		Online purchase
5/6/2012	Google - Google storage		Online purchase
29/4/2012	Google Apps - Domain Registration betterspreadbetting.com		Online purchase
5/6/2011	Google - Google storage		Online purchase

Multiple Google Accounts

I like to have at least two Google accounts, so that I can separate my personal and business activities and so that I can have different personal and business email addresses. Therefore, I sometimes need to log into two different accounts simultaneously on the same chromebook or another device.

On your **Account settings** page you will see an option to allow **Multiple sign-in**, which by default should be switched off. Clicking the link marked **Edit** will take you to the page shown below. You can use it to switch the Multiple sign-in feature **On** once you have read the various warnings; these warnings being there mainly to advise you that you may get confused and end up doing things in the wrong account.

.

Once you have enabled multiple sign-in you can switch between your accounts by pulling down the menu of options attached to your user name (i.e. yourname@gmail.com) at the top-right of your Gmail or Google Docs session.

Choose the **Switch account** or **Sign in to another account** option (not shown) to switch to one of your other accounts, and see how it opens a new browser tab with your alternate identity.

Personally, I prefer to do this a slightly different way by opening a new browser window (click the wrench icon and choose **New window**) so that my two identities are kept completely separate in entirely different windows. Even better, when working on a traditional Windows PC I prefer to log into my two Google Accounts (personal and business) using two entirely different web browsers: Google Chrome, and Microsoft Internet Explorer respectively.

Multiple Accounts on Your Chromebook or Chromebox

What I just described is a necessary way of "switching context" between Google Accounts when running the Chrome web browser on a PC that takes an age to switch between real users. Since the chromebook allows you to sign out of one account and into another quite quickly via the initial sign-on screen, and since those separate user accounts are tied absolutely to particular Google Accounts in the Chrome web browser, I actually find it much easier – and less confusing – to switch between accounts in this way when operating a chromebook.

Multiple Chromebook Users

Note that unless you expressly forbid it, anyone with a Google Account can login via your chromebook. It's nothing to worry about, and all part of the plan, because the whole point is that (theoretically, at least) anyone can access their Google account, apps and settings via any Chrome device anywhere. Which includes you, if you happen to lose your chromebook or its gets damaged, in which case you can get up-and-running again really quickly by finding a friend with a chromebook or by going out and buying another one. It's not like the old days when, if you lost or damaged your PC, you'd have lost all of the files and programs stored on it.

If you do want to restrict the users that can log into your chromebook, or if you want to disable the guest browsing feature, you can do so by clicking the **Manage other users** button on the Settings web page at **chrome://settings/accounts** as shown here:

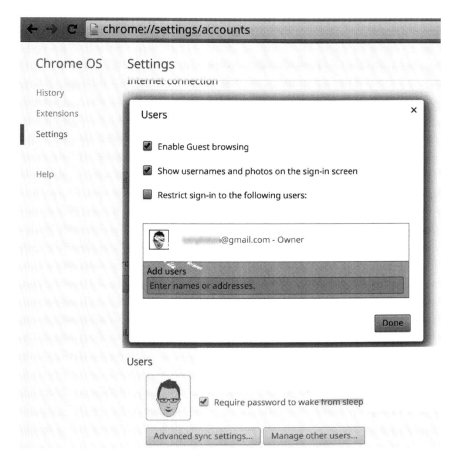

Chapter Summary

I have described what a chromebook is, how you sign in to it and how you interact with it via the keyboard and screen. I have also described how to move files between the built-in storage, any plugged-in storage (such as a USB stick or SD card), and the Google Drive that will be introduced more formally in a later chapter.

I have described the Chrome web browser that underpins all of the apps that run on your chromebook, plus your Google account that underpins everything you do on the chromebook while also acting as the linchpin that connects your settings and data across Chrome browser sessions on different devices at different times. Via your Google Account you can set your security and storage preferences.

It is just about possible to utilize multiple Google accounts (different identities, if you have them) within a single Chrome browser session on your PC; but it is more effective to keep these accounts entirely separate by signing into your chromebook as different users—which is both fast and effective.

Before we continue, now might be a good time to remind you not to forget to redeem your Google Goodies. At the time of writing, my brand new Chromebook Pixel came with an offer of a massive 1TB of free Google Drive data storage for two years (I thought it was meant to be three) redeemable at:
http://www.google.com/intl/en/chrome/devices/goodies.html

Some people believe the 1TB data storage offer alone to be worth the price of the Chromebook Pixel, but beware that if you continue to use it after the two or three years... you'll have to pay for it!

Find more **chromebook resources** including **books, chromebook computers** (if you don't already have one) and **compatible printers** at usa.thechromebook.info or uk.thechromebook.info.

---

4 - Web Apps and the Chrome Web Store

Just as the Apple iPad has its iTunes store, and just as Android phones have the Android Market, so Chrome has the Chrome Web Store from where you can install web apps. These web apps, which were originally mostly just packaged web sites rather than locally installable programs, are not necessarily chromebook-specific and in many cases can be utilized just as effectively when running via the Chrome web browser on your traditional PC.

The Web Store also offers a large number of Chrome browser extensions, which act more like installable utility programs or browser plug-ins. These extensions might perform local tasks – like interacting with your computer hardware – which remotely running web apps cannot perform.

You can visit the Chrome Web Store by clicking the app icon of that name or by typing https://chrome.google.com/webstore into the Chrome browser's address bar.

Example Apps

I'll now present you with a few example apps that may be installed from the Chrome Web Store, simply to whet your appetite for beginning your own voyage of discovery.

Kindle Cloud Reader

I will use the Kindle Cloud Reader as my first example app—in part because I like it, and in part because it shows that you don't have to (although you might want to) use Google's own equivalent book reader.

In the following picture you can see how I have located the **Cloud Reader** app in the Web Store, and installed it so that it may henceforth be launched from the **Apps** menu.

Actually, it's not as simple as that. For some bizarre reason I find it almost impossible to find the Kindle Cloud reader in the Chrome Web Store simply by searching, and in fact I found it by accident by performing a Google search for "cloud reader" and clicking on the entry titled Chrome Web Store. I can save you the trouble, hopefully, by directing you to:

https://chrome.google.com/webstore/detail/cloud-reader/icdipabjmbhpdkjaihfjoikhjjeneebd

Alternatively, you might access the Kindle Cloud Reader simply by visiting http://read.amazon.com. However you get there, this is what the Kindle Cloud Reader looks like when viewing the third edition of this book:

The good news is that this app gives you access to your entire library of purchased Kindle books plus the Kindle Store itself on your chromebook (or PC or any other compatible device with a Chrome web browser). The bad news is that it doesn't seem to respond to "swiping" actions on the Chromebook Pixel touchscreen... which would have been a nice way to turn the pages.

At this point I have to say that I actually prefer reading e-books in PDF format via Google Play Books, because they can be viewed "as printed" rather than in the free-flowing page-less style of Kindle books. But it's a personal preference.

Pixlr

As someone who engages in creative pursuits, for example designing book covers, a good image editing application is essential for me. But there really is no need for me to invest in the bona fide complete Adobe Photoshop application; therefore previously I have relied on the free PAINT.NET Windows application for my image editing needs. Obviously I can't use this particular application on my chromebook (or Adobe Photoshop for that matter) so I have a real requirement to find a good image editing application in the Chrome Web Store.

I found exactly what I needed in the form of the **Pixlr** web app, which looks and feels remarkably like the PAINT.NET application that I was already used to and which serves *all my needs* for image editing including manipulating multi-layered images.

In my later case study chapter you will see how I used the Google Drawing tool to compose a cover for the book you are reading now. I could have used Pixlr instead, and in future... I probably will. For our purposes right here right now, I'm content to use Pixlr to *improve* the cover design that I created.

My requirement in this case was quite simple: to take the cover design that I had already created and saved in JPG format, and to load it up into Pixlr so that I could recolor some of the letters in the book title, as shown here:

Note that I have encountered a problem with the Pixlr web app, which is the apparent inability to save the edited image to **My computer**. Having resorted temporarily to workaround solutions such as saving the image to my **Picasa** account (which is one of the other options) and downloading from there, I then discovered what the real problem was: it is only possible to save your work to the **Downloads** folder on your chromebook rather than saving directly to one of your **Google Drive** folders. So now I just save edited images to my **Downloads** folder and use the **Files** app to copy to the intended destination in my **Google Drive**.

Text <txt>

Do you remember the Microsoft Windows simple text editor called Notepad? I found it surprisingly useful: not for storing and arranging notes (for which there are better applications), but for transferring unformatted text from one application to another. And it's the same with the **Text <txt>** that you can find in the Chrome Web Store at https://chrome.google.com/webstore/detail/text/mmfbcljfglbokpmkim bfghdkjmjhdgbg.

To see what I mean: try highlighting some text on a web page, copy it by pressing **ctrl + c**, and then paste it into a Google Docs document by pressing **ctrl + v**. See how the font and format of the text is retained when pasted, which – frankly – I often don't want. Now try pasting into the **Text <txt>** app, copying again (**ctrl + c**), and then pasting again (**ctrl + v**). This time only the plain text will be pasted.

By focusing on my real but slightly contrived requirement, I'm not doing this app justice. It can also be used to type notes on the chromebook when you're offline (not connected to the Internet), and it can be used as a HTML code editor.

Apps vs. Extensions (and Packaged Apps)

I've already hinted that there is a difference between apps (which historically have been glorified web sites) and extensions (which are locally-installed programs rather like browser plug-ins). It used to be the case that the Chrome Web Store made an explicit distinction between Apps and Extensions, but now the distinction is less obvious.

Perhaps the best way to understand the difference between apps and extensions is to think of apps as distinct browser destinations that provide specific functionality – like editing documents or checking the financial news – whereas extensions enhance the features of the Chrome web browser across apps and websites. So, for example, you might install the **ChromeVox** extension that allows the web browser to speak the content of any web site that you visit.

I have to admit that I became weary of the ChromeVox constant chatter after a while; in which context you will be pleased to know that it is easy to disable or even remove specific browser extensions via the **Extensions** category of the **Chrome Settings**. Like this:

Chrome OS   Extensions

History

| Extensions

Settings

ChromeVox   1.23.0
ChromeVox - Giving Voice to Chrome Visit website

☐ Allow in incognito Options

☐ Developer mode

☑ Enabled

A different extension, which may not have universal appeal but which appeals to me personally, is the IG extension that allows financial traders to place deals relating to the companies and stock indices that are mentioned on websites such as Reuters and Bloomberg. This is another good example of an extension that works across web sites by extracting information, e.g. company names, from whatever website you happen to be viewing at the time; and it looks like this (extension pulled down at the right):

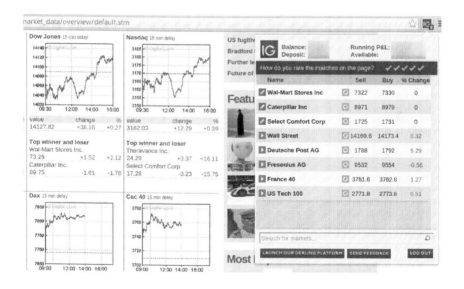

For completeness, I should tell you that there is a third class of installable component that blurs the boundary between web apps and extensions; this is the *packaged app*. While web apps (also known as *hosted apps*) are basically wrappers for existing web sites, *packaged apps* are downloaded and locally-installed apps that can function even when the user is offline. The latter are similar to the "apps" that you are used to installing on your mobile phone.

As if this wasn't complicating matters enough, Google has introduced Native Client technology which provides locally installed applications greater access to the hardware of the underlying computer (i.e. the chromebook or the PC running the Chrome web browser). One of the first fruits of this development is the Microsoft-compatible QuickOffice suite introduced in chapter *8 – A Quick Look at QuickOffice*.

Personally I think that the introduction of packaged apps and native clients goes against the original spirit of Chrome OS providing lightweight web access as a pure thin client. With these installable apps and the PC-like desktop the chromebook is looking and behaving more and more like a traditional PC all the time, which of course may be necessary in order to attract more users. It's also beginning to look more and more like the Android operating system that provides a desktop of sorts along with a suite of installable apps plus a web browser; and this may be no accident because Google is known to be considering merging its two operating systems (Chrome OS and Android) at some point in the future.

Themes

In addition to apps and extensions, the Chrome Web Store also offers browser **Themes**. These made perfect sense in the early days when the Chrome web browser occupied the whole of the chromebook screen, but are not so compelling now that chromebooks have a PC-style "desktop" that is unaffected by these in-browser themes. Still, they provide a way to add a little sparkle to your browsing session—for example by installing the metallic "Brushed" theme as shown below.

In the following screenshot I have killed two birds with one stone by showing what another Chrome theme looks like while also demonstrating an additional chromebook feature: the ability to perform rudimentary image manipulations – in this case cropping – on any images you open on the chromebook.

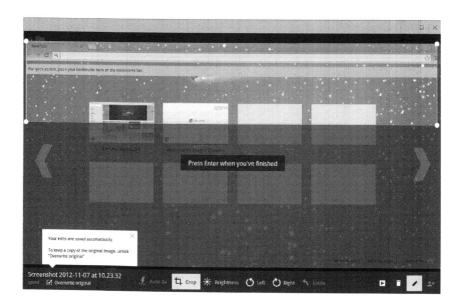

Don't Forget the Preloaded Apps

It's worth reiterating at this point that when you fire up your chromebook for the first time you will find that several apps are already available via the **Apps** icon on the launchbar at the bottom of the screen. So when you locate the Google Play Books app (for example) in the Chrome Web Store, you should find that you don't need to install it because it is already installed; and it's the same story with Google Maps.

One of the newer pre-installed apps is the Keep note-taking app that you can see pictured in action below. It allows you to write color-code notes and lists—the latter allowing you to strike off items as having been completed. Most importantly, these notes are stored on your Google Drive at http://drive.google.com/keep and they are searchable.

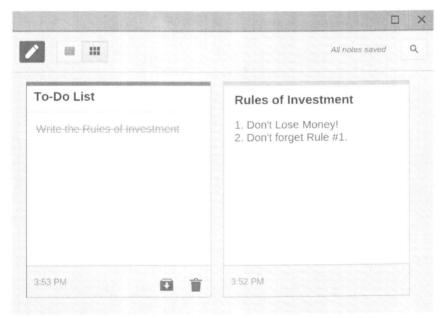

I do have one bugbear to vent off about. In an earlier edition of this book, I presented Scratchpad as the chromebook's default note-taking app. I have also been known to use the Gmail Tasks list for recording pending and completed tasks. It seems that the Keep app has superseded both of these forerunner facilities. My bugbear is that I sometimes wish Google wouldn't "innovate" quite so quickly by devising new apps while letting others fall by the wayside.

Not Just for Chromebooks and Chromeboxes

The Chrome Web Store is not only home to apps, extensions and themes for your chromebook or chromebox, but also home to apps and extensions for the Chrome web browser running on your PC—if you still have one.

The World Wide Web Store

So the Google chromebook has its very own web store boasting "thousands of apps", just like the app stores provided for Apple and Android users. But there is an even bigger web store in the form of the worldwide web that you have been using for all these years. Just because a web site doesn't have an icon in the Chrome Web Store, it doesn't mean you can't use the functionality provided by that web site via the Chrome web browser on your chromebook. I would argue that the World Wide Web Store is the biggest app store in the world.

What do you want to do today?

Publish a book? Just point your Chrome web browser in the direction of http://www.createspace.com or http://kdp.amazon.com.

Send and receive money (including e-commerce payments) over the internet? Just point your Chrome web browser in the direction of http://www.paypal.com.

Manage your company or personal accounts? Simply head over to http://quickbooksonline.intuit.com or (in this case) find the web app in the Chrome Web Store.

Note that these websites will be used as demonstration vehicles in my later case study.

Chapter Summary

Just as most mobile phones have their respective online stores for media and apps, so the Chrome web browser has its own Chrome Web Store for hosted apps, packaged apps, extensions and themes. You also have access to the functionality provided by all of the existing web sites you have been using already.

Find more **chromebook resources** including **books, chromebook computers** (if you don't already have one) and **compatible printers** at usa.thechromebook.info or uk.thechromebook.info.

5 - Social Apps

When you think of Google, many of you – when not thinking about the search engine – will think of applications like Gmail and Google Calendar. I call these "social apps" because you use them to interact with other people by emailing them (Gmail) or scheduling meetings with them (Google Calendar). We can add to this list the more obvious social apps such as the Google+ social network (i.e. Google's answer to Facebook) and the Google Hangouts app that lets you video call people or chat with them.

So this chapter will focus of some of the social features of the Chrome OS and the wider Google ecosystem.

Gmail

When you initiate the Gmail application via its shortcut – or by typing **mail.google.com** into your web browser's address bar – you will notice at the top of the browser page, a ribbon of links to various Google apps like this:

| Search | Images | Maps | Play | YouTube | News | **Gmail** | Drive | Calendar | More ▾ |

If you're not already using Gmail, the chances are good that you're using another web-based email provider like Yahoo! Mail or Hotmail. While it is possible to continue using these providers, and there is even a Yahoo! Mail App for Chrome, you might like to consider migrating to Gmail so that Google becomes your one-stop-shop with a single sign-in for email, calendar (discussed next) and documents on your PC, chromebook and

Android mobile phone. If you like the sound of it, you'll need some help with migrating to Gmail.

Migrating to Gmail (optional)

You already have a Google account that you used to log into your chromebook, so you already have a Gmail address which will be of the form *yourgoogleaccountname@gmail.com*. What you don't yet have is access to the messages still flowing into your old email address; the messages you will need to see until you have notified all of your contacts that you have changed your email address. And what you don't yet know, which may be different from how your existing email interface works, is how to arrange your Gmail messages into a folder-like structure using labels. Let's look at each of these aspects in turn.

First, let's look at channeling messages from your old email address through to the Gmail interface. You don't have to do this, because you could simply keep logging into your old email account to check for new messages—for example by typing http://mail.live.com into the Chrome web browser's omnibox so as to access your Microsoft Hotmail account. But I think it helps with the transition to cloud computing with the chromebook if you move decisively to Gmail as your single email application.

There are two ways in which you can channel incoming email messages from your old provider to Gmail. The first way is to forward the incoming messages, which I can demonstrate using the Yahoo! Mail **POP & Forwarding** options shown below. Notice that I have checked the option to **Forward your (BT) Yahoo! Mail** and I have entered my new Gmail email address.

POP & Forwarding

○ Allow your BT Yahoo! Mail to be POPed 🔳

When POPing my messages, | don't POP spam. | ▾ |

◉ Forward your BT Yahoo! Mail 🔳

Forward mail to the following address, | mygoogleacccount@gmai |

[e.g., user@company.com]

(Note that this setting is at the Yahoo! end rather than at the Gmail end)

The forwarding technique allows your old email provider to push incoming messages into your Gmail account. The other technique is for Gmail to pull the incoming messages from your old account, the key to which is also contained in the figure above. Notice how I could have checked the option to **Allow your (BT) Yahoo! Mail to be POPed** instead, in which case I would also need to do something in my Gmail account so as to actually do the *POPing*.

Clicking the small cog wheel ⚙ at the top-right of your Gmail screen initiates a pull-down menu from which you can select the option to adjust your **Settings**. On the **Settings** page you can select the **Accounts and Import** tab in order to set up one or more Post Office Protocol (POP) accounts within the **Check email from other accounts** section of the page... as shown below.

Check email from other accounts (using POP3):
Learn more

▓▓▓@gmail.com
Last checked: 0 minutes ago. View history Check mail now

▓▓▓@btinternet.com
Last checked: 0 minutes ago. View history Check mail now

▓▓▓@btinternet.com
Last checked: 0 minutes ago. View history Check mail now

Add a POP3 mail account you own

You can see that the 'old' email accounts I have set up for POPing are checked periodically, and you can set up a new legacy account by clicking the link labeled **Add a POP3 mail account you own**. You will be guided through the setup process which will ask for your old email address (from which the correct settings will be determined automatically) and will send an email to your old email address containing a verification code that you will need to enter in order to complete the process. In case you haven't figured it out, the verification step is to ensure that you really do own the old email account and that you are not fetching someone else's private correspondence into your Inbox.

On the subject of your **Inbox**; this is where any new emails to your old email address will now appear unless you decide to 'label' them as part of the setup process. This brings us nicely to the concept of labeling your email messages.

Labeling Email Messages

Many web-based email providers allow you to move messages from your **Inbox** into specific folders. Gmail allows you to do a similar thing by labeling your messages as shown below. You can see in this example how I have applied the **Personal** and **Work** labels to three of the messages in my **Inbox** using the **Labels** drop-down menu. You can also see how I could **Create new** labels and **Manage labels**.

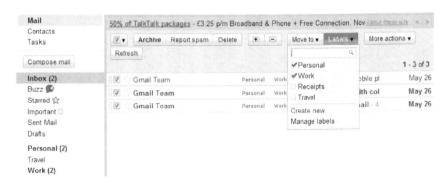

It is possible to nest labels within labels so as to create a hierarchy (how about **Personal / 2010** and **Personal / 2011** and so on?) and you should have figured out from my example that any message can be given more than one label. By selecting the **Personal** label (in the far left column) I will be able to filter all messages labeled **Personal**, for example, regardless of which other labels are applied to those messages.

So you can label your messages, but they will still clog up your Inbox, won't they? You can move them out of the Inbox using the **Move to** drop-down menu that you can see in the above figure. Although the effect is similar to moving a message to a new or existing label, I think that this particular option might be better named **Move from**, because it disconnects the message from whichever labeled folder you are viewing and moves it to the new or existing label while retaining all other labels. So in my example, the effect of moving my already-labeled messages to the **Travel** label would be to remove the **Inbox** label while retaining the existing **Personal** and **Work** labels in addition to the new **Travel** label. So I didn't so much move the message *to* **Travel** as move it *from* the **Inbox**.

Composing Email Messages with Google Drive Attachments

One of the things that I found strange in the early stages of the chromebook story was the fact that in order to attach a file stored in your Google Drive (see chapter *6 - Google Drive*), to a message that you were composing using Gmail, you had to first download the file to the Downloads folder. This seemed to be an unnecessary step, and not consistent with the cloud computing ethos.

It is now possible to attach a Google Drive file directly to an email message, as shown here:

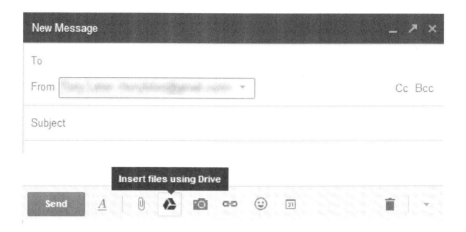

If you don't see the **Insert files using Drive** option, it may be because you're using the old Gmail compose facility; in which case you should see a clickable link near the top-right of your Gmail screen that states "**Try out the new compose experience**".

Note that you have always been able to **Share** individual Google Drive files directly via email without downloading them, and you can learn more about Google Drive in chapter *6 - Google Drive*.

Contacts and Chat

Not so many years ago, weren't you just sick of typing all your contacts into your mobile phone and then having to retype them when you changed phones? For the more technical readers: weren't you sick of syncing the contacts between your web-mail provider, the email application on your PC, and your mobile phone, only to find that some contacts had gone missing in transit or had their 'home' and 'mobile' numbers mysteriously switched around?

Let's keep it really simple then, by using your Google contacts list as the central repository for all your contacts. Watch how they magically get synced with the Contacts application on your Android mobile phone... and never get lost. Watch how there is no third contacts list stored on your PC, because your chromebook simply accesses the contacts list in the Gmail web app via the Chrome browser.

You can access the Gmail contacts application by clicking the **Gmail** pull-down at the top-right of your Gmail session, and then clicking the **Contacts** item.

To get you off to a flying start, why don't you import your existing contacts, once only, from your Yahoo! Mail or Microsoft Outlook by choosing **Import** from the drop-down menu of **More actions**? You will need to have used the export function of your previous email / contacts program first.

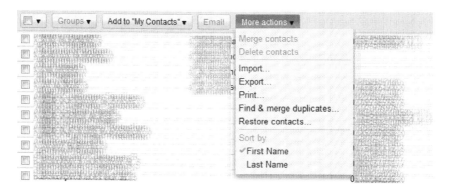

About Google Chat

The reason you have the contacts is, of course, so that you can contact them... and not just by email. Skype users will be well versed in contacting their contacts via instant messages, voice calls, and video calls. You can do the same things from within Gmail.

In the lower left corner of your regular Gmail window you should see a list of people with whom you can "chat", and if not, just click the **Chat** icon as shown below. Clicking any name in this list will launch a "chat" window via which you can send instant messages to the selected person; or click one of the icons in the chat window to make a voice or video call.

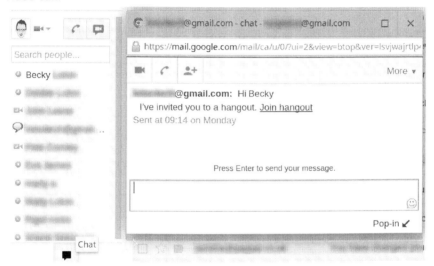

Note that you can also do something very similar by launching the ***Google+ Hangout*** *app from the chromebook launcher bar at the bottom of the screen.*

Gmail Offline

As a further step towards making chromebooks useable when not connected to the Internet, Google offers a Gmail Offline application that is available in the Chrome Web Store. Although this app runs within a browser window, it provides a user interface not unlike traditional email clients like Microsoft Outlook (from what I remember) with the ability to read and compose messages when no internet connection is available.

Google Calendar

All good Personal Information Management (PIM) software such as Microsoft Outlook, every good web-based email provider, and all good mobile phone operating systems offer a calendar application to complement the *email* and *contacts* applications. Google provides a popular calendar application that you can access in at least three ways: either type **calendar.google.com** into your web browser's address bar, or click the application shortcut (if you've installed the web app), or click the link displayed in the ribbon at the top of your Gmail session.

Google Calendar provides all of the calendar functionality you are likely to need. You can set up multiple calendars—maybe one for business, and one for personal appointments. You can invite your friends or colleagues to events that you schedule in your calendar, and you can even access your friends' calendars (if they let you). You can view calendars by day, week, or month, and you can subscribe to calendar feeds from other calendars such as the **UK Holidays** calendar feed as shown below.

If you're migrating to Google Calendar from another calendar application you will be pleased to know that you won't have to retype all of your existing entries. Just click the **Add** link that you can see at the bottom-left of the previous figure, and browse for an **iCal** or **CSV** file that you have exported from Microsoft Outlook, Yahoo! Calendar, or whichever calendar application you used previously.

Don't forget that, because the Google Calendar is entirely web based, you can access your calendar from any computer anywhere as long as it has a web browser.

Synchronized with Android

One of the most useful features of the Google mail, contacts and calendar suite is that it synchronizes automatically with those same apps on your Android mobile phone – providing you use the same Google Account on each device. Enter a new contact or calendar entry via your PC, chromebook, or Android phone and see it synced automatically on all the other devices. Gone are the days when you had to do a three-way-sync between your mobile phone, Microsoft Outlook running on your PC, and your online email or calendar provided by Yahoo! or Google—so no more important meetings or contacts need go astray.

Google+

I have to admit that I'm not much of a social networker. Well, not in the virtual sense, anyway. But it would be remiss of me not to mention Google's own Google+ social network. I'll leave you to begin your social networking journey by launching the Google+ app or by visiting http://plus.google.com.

Chapter Summary

In this chapter I have introduced a subset of Chrome apps that support social activities; i.e. interacting with other people via email, chats and video calls, scheduled meetings, and social networking. In the next-but-one chapter I will introduce another subset of Chrome apps for creating documents of various kinds, but we first need to look at the Google Drive cloud-based file system as the storage system for those documents.

Find more **chromebook resources** including **books**, **chromebook computers** (if you don't already have one) and **compatible printers** at usa.thechromebook.info or uk.thechromebook.info.

.

the chrome book

6 - Google Drive

In the cloud computing model, all of your documents and other files are stored "in the cloud" on a server computer at the other end of your Internet connection, rather than being stored locally on your PC hard drive. The idea is that you can access your files anytime from anywhere using any device that has an Internet connection and which runs the Chrome web browser.

In the Google cloud computing world, the home to your files on the Internet is the Google Drive that is associated with your Google account.

Navigating the Google Drive

You can access your Google Drive by clicking the **Drive** option on your Google account menu bar displayed at the top of the web browser when you're in Gmail or Google Calendar, or you can click the triangular Google Drive app icon on your chromebook, or you can simply type **drive.google.com** into the Chrome web browser's omnibox (web address bar).

As shown in the next figure, you can navigate your Google Drive folders in the left-hand column and see the contents of the currently-selected **Folder** (previously called a **Collection**) to the right—which is very much the same as when operating a local file explorer such as Windows Explorer, except that this file explorer is on the web. In this example I have selected a **Collection** (the new term being **Folder**) named **Business** which contains a Google spreadsheet named **Test Spreadsheet** (imaginative, eh?) and a sub-collection named **NOTES**.

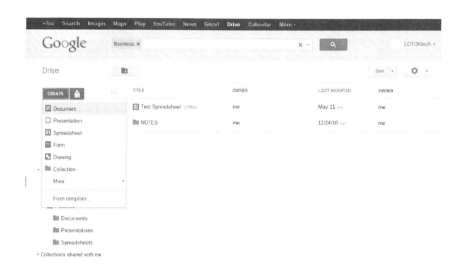

You can use the **CREATE** button, or right-click a specific folder, in order to create a new file—which might be a **Document**, **Presentation**, **Spreadsheet**, **Form**, **Drawing** or **Collection** (i.e. **Folder**). Note that the documents, presentations and spreadsheets that you create here will be in Google's own web-based format rather than in the hitherto industry-standard Microsoft Office format; but it is possible to *export to* and *import from* the Microsoft Office equivalent formats. Further guidance on creating and editing these Google Docs files is given in the next chapter.

When using the web-based Google Drive you can perform the kinds of file manipulation tasks that you are used to; for example, dragging files from one folder to another or renaming files (by right-clicking and choosing **Rename** from the pop-up context menu).

Using the Google Drive to Store Non-Google Files

Just like Microsoft's rival SkyDrive, you can use your Google Drive to store or backup any or all of your files on the web, even if they're not Google documents or spreadsheets.

To upload a file to your Google Drive, all you need to do is click the upload icon shown circled in the following screenshot and then select the required file from the PC or chromebook file system (e.g. your chromebook **Downloads** folder or an attached USB stick). Be sure to have selected the required Google Drive destination folder / collection first.

As shown above, when you upload a non-Google file to your Google Drive you are given the option to convert the file to a corresponding Google Docs format file (if there is one); for example to convert a Microsoft Word document to a Google Docs document. As a general rule, I tend to upload without conversion so that the file is kept as-is and is merely *stored* on my Google Drive.

Accessing Your Google Drive

You can access your web-based Google Drive from any computer or other device that runs a web browser; ideally Google Chrome. But on specific devices such as the chromebook (or chromebox) and your Windows PC there are other ways of interacting with the Google Drive.

Google Drive on Your Chromebook

You can access your Google Drive on the web via your chromebook either by typing **drive.google.com** into a browser tab or by selecting the **Google Drive** app icon as shown in the previous chapter.

You can also access your Google Drive on your chromebook via the **Files** app as shown in the previous chapter, which provides a convenient way for you to copy files such as pictures and other non-Google files to your online Google Drive from another source such as a USB stick or from your Downloads folder.

Note that when you access your Google Drive via the file manager, you may not automatically be able to open a file from your Google Drive when you are offline (not connected to the Internet) until you have marked the file as **Available offline**. You need to be online in order to mark files as available offline – so that they can be automatically copied to your chromebook – but of course this should not be necessary for files that originated on your chromebook in the first place. Depending on the version of the Chrome OS on your chromebook, you may need to check a checkbox (as shown below) or you may need to open the file's context menu (right-click, two-finger tap, or long press) and choose the **Available offline** item.

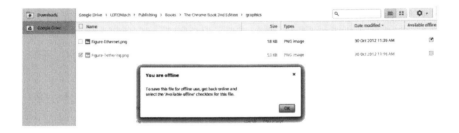

The plot thickens. In the following figure you can see that when attempting to open a Google Docs (.gdoc) document via the chromebook file manager, I receive an error message that "**You must be online to access this file**"...

..and yet, when I access exactly the same document via the chromebook web browser I find that it is correctly flagged as being available **Offline** (see picture below) such that I have no problems opening it in Google Drive's "offline" mode discussed later in this chapter.

Don't worry if this is a little confusing – it is for me, too – but you get used to it after a while. At this point I just wanted to make you aware that accessing your Google Drive via the chromebook **Files** app is not exactly equivalent to accessing your Google Drive via the Chrome web browser.

Google Drive on Your PC

I've already told you that you can use your online Google Drive to store any of your data files; and these files might be Microsoft Office files such as Word documents or Excel spreadsheets.

It can be a bit of a pain uploading these files to your Google Drive via the web interface, so Google have provided an easier way for you to synchronize your Windows PC file system with the Google Drive online storage.

Download and Configure Google Drive

You can **Download Google Drive** to your Windows PC by clicking the link shown below, which should appear in the left column of your online Google Drive.

Once you've downloaded and installed the program, you can configure it to synchronize any or all of your Google Drive folders with your PC. You will also be able to change the synchronize settings at any time by right-clicking the triangular Google Drive icon on the Windows taskbar and selecting **Preferences** from the pop-up menu as shown below.

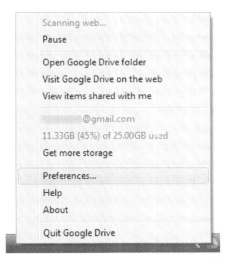

Choosing which folders to synchronize is important, because the contents of your chosen folders will be downloaded to your PC—which will take both time and broadband bandwidth. You might want to synchronize a folder containing the document(s) you are currently working on, but not the folder containing your lifetime collection of photographs.

Using Google Drive on Your PC

As part of the installation and configuration you will have chosen the location of a new Google Drive folder on your PC hard disk, and you can access this Google Drive folder via the Windows File Explorer... like this:

This provides a very convenient way of backing up your important files on the web. Just copy your Microsoft Office document files or other files to the Google Drive folder, or save them directly there, and you will see them magically copied to your online Google Drive for safekeeping. It's a lot easier than burning backup DVDs and finding a safe place to store them, isn't it?

Personally, I would be using this PC Google Drive facility even if I didn't own a chromebook, to ensure that my important PC files were automatically "backed up" online. In this respect I tend to regard the Google Drive folder of my PC hard drive as my entire hard drive as far as my data files are concerned, and I ignore the rest of my PC hard drive except as somewhere to install software.

The Microsoft Word Auto-Save Problem

It may be just me, but at one point I ran into a problem when the Google Drive program was set to run all the time on my PC. The problem was that some of my Microsoft Word files became 'unsyncable', which I put down to the fact that Word was trying to auto-save my work at the same time that Google Drive was trying to sync it to the cloud.

This may no longer be a problem, but to solve it initially I tended to have the Google Drive program switched off on my PC while editing Microsoft Word documents, and I ran the Google Drive program manually at regular intervals (at least once per day) to back up the Word documents and other files that I have saved to my Google Drive folder. This approach to backing up to Google Drive was still much easier than the old method of backing up the important documents on my PC by burning CDs or DVDs.

Google Drive on Mac, iPhone / iPad, and Android

In addition to using Google Drive via the web and on your Windows PC or chromebook, it is also possible to install Google Drive on your Mac computer, on your iPhone / iPad, or on your Android mobile phone or tablet.

I'm not a user of Apple products, so I can't offer any assistance with the Mac version of Google Drive which I assume operates rather like the Windows PC version. Similarly, I can't help you with the iPhone / iPad version, but I am able to tell you something about the Android mobile phone version.

In the following screenshot I am showing two things in one. I'm showing the files and folders visible via the Google Drive app on my Android mobile phone, and I'm also showing how a screenshot of this (taken on the phone itself) can itself be copied just like any other file by tapping the triangular Google Drive icon that you can see at the top-right of the picture. I use this facility all the time to get photos from my phone camera onto my Google Drive for safe storage at the tap of a button.

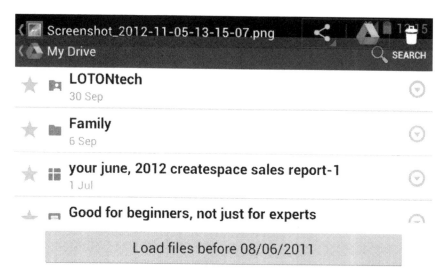

When operating Google Drive on your Android phone you can make files available offline on a one-by-one basis so that your entire online archive does not eat up all of your phone's memory; which brings us to...

Offline Docs

One of the issues with the original web-based Google Docs office suite was the fact that you had to be online in order to edit your documents. Having no Internet connection on your chromebook meant that you had no access to your documents; and a lost Internet connection while editing a document meant that your changes would be lost. Google has gone some way to addressing this limitation by creating an Offline Docs facility.

In the Chrome browser, scroll down the left-hand column and expand the **More** item to reveal the **Offline** option as shown in the screenshot below. You will need to install the **Drive Chrome** web app onto your system if you don't already have it, and you'll need to click the **Enable Offline** button shown on this page.

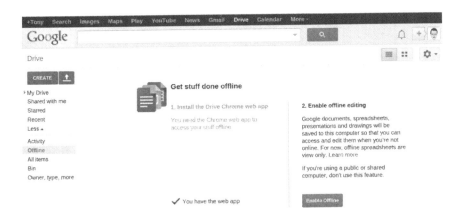

Upon enabling offline editing, you will see that your **Google documents, spreadsheets and presentations are being synced for offline editing** as shown below.

IMPORTANT NOTE: Only enable Offline Docs on your own personal computer, and not on a public or shared computer! You don't want those documents to be accessible to anyone else in your local library or Internet café.

Whenever you access your Google Drive via the Chrome web browser, via the triangular Google Drive app icon, or simply by visiting **drive.google.com**, you will be able to edit your Google documents (or view your Google spreadsheets) whether you are online or offline. It should be pretty seamless because the Chrome web browser will detect whether or not you have an Internet connection, and will put you into online or offline mode as appropriate. Any changes that you make offline will be synced to your online Google Drive when your Internet connection is restored.

Only Applies to Google Docs

Note that this Offline Docs feature only applies to your Google-format documents. If you've downloaded the Google Drive software to sync your saved files to and from the cloud for safe keeping, you can always edit your regular Microsoft Word documents (or Excel spreadsheets, or anything else) on your PC and have them backed automatically via Google Drive when you're next connected to the Internet.

Note also that at the time of writing, only Google Docs documents are fully editable offline, and your Google spreadsheets can be viewed offline but not edited. I'm writing these words right now in a Google Document while offline, as you can see from the text in the screenshot below ... but I had to go online to insert the picture, even though it was stored in my local Downloads folder.

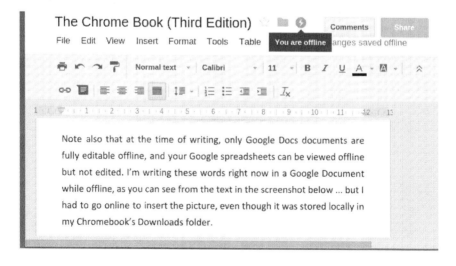

91

Where you have an intermittent Internet connection, your Google Document session should switch automatically between online and offline mode. You should be able to continue typing when your connection drops, and benefit from the fact that changes are saved offline until the connection is restored and you see (at the top of your document) the reassuring message: **All changes saved in Drive**.

Chapter Summary

In this chapter I have introduced the Google Drive cloud-based online storage; how you navigate it and how you can use it to create and arrange the Google-format documents and presentations that will be described in more detail in the next chapter. I have also explained how you can use Google Drive to store or back-up your non-Google files such as Microsoft Office documents, and in this context I have explained how Google Drive interoperates with the local file system of your chromebook, PC, Android mobile phone or other device. Finally, I explained how Google Drive can be configured to allow offline editing of Google Docs files, these files being the subject of the next chapter.

Find more **chromebook resources** including **books**, **chromebook computers** (if you don't already have one) and **compatible printers** at usa.thechromebook.info or uk.thechromebook.info.

---

7 - Google Drive Documents

In the previous chapter I told you about Google Drive, and how it is possible to use its web interface to create new Google-format documents, spreadsheets, presentations and other files in your drive. This ability to create and edit various "office" (with a small "o", not Microsoft Office) documents is what used to be known as Google Docs—before they changed the name of the whole shebang to Google Drive.

In this chapter I'll dig a little deeper into what might be described as the Google "office suite". It's the office suite that you'll be using by default on your web-only chromebook, but it's not the only option as you will discover towards the end of the chapter and in the next.

Document

The first and most useful office file type that you can create in your Google Drive using Google Docs is the "Google Doc"...or Document. As a freelance writer for several publications, I have written numerous structured (i.e. with headings) feature articles, and shared the end results with editors directly via the web, without going anywhere near Microsoft Word. I even wrote the entire first and most of the third edition of this book as a Google Document.

Will Google Docs Suit Your Needs (and Mine)?

As an e-book creation tool, the Google Docs word processor is perfectly acceptable. As a tool for writing linear articles with alternating text and pictures, it is perfectly acceptable. But as a tool for producing professionally formatted book manuscripts and converting these to print-ready Portable Document Format (PDF) files for publication in paperback format, it may not be quite up to the job... yet. *But wait for my case study chapter for the final judgment.*

As a professional publisher of books, I do still sometimes need the very advanced features of Microsoft Word when typesetting manuscripts for publication; but in the previous chapter I showed how Word documents can be stored in Google Drive, and in my later chapter *10 - Cloud Computing Conundrums* I will show how it is possible to run Microsoft Word and other Windows programs remotely from a legacy PC using the chromebook screen and keyboard.

Personally, I can spend perhaps 90% of my time "in the cloud" writing a base manuscript and benefiting from the automatic backups provided by Google Drive; but I usually have to come out of the cloud for the remaining 10% of the time to "finish off" using Microsoft Word or another more comprehensive tool. It's easy enough to do because Google Drive allows me to export my almost-complete manuscript in the widely interchangeable Microsoft Word (.docx) format.

What Can Google Docs Do for You?

Having set your expectations at a suitably low level; let me now tell you what you can achieve with a Google Docs document. As just stated, I wrote the first edition of this book as a Google Document, and for e-books I can tell you that it works pretty well. As proof, the following figure shows a section of the original book manuscript (as a Google Document) comprising a styled heading followed by alternating text and graphics. You can also see in this figure how one of my colleagues has commented on the document using the collaboration features of Google Docs that will be discussed shortly.

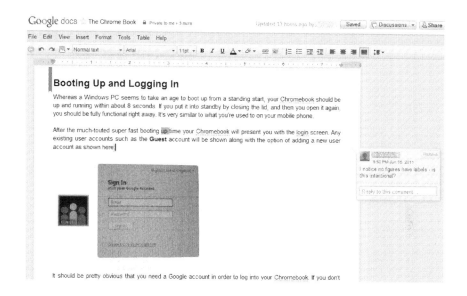

Even though *you* may be moving to "the cloud", not everyone else will have done so just yet, so some people – like the magazine editors with whom I work – will still be expecting you to provide them with documents in Microsoft Word format. You can convert any Google Docs document to Microsoft Word (.docx) format and other popular formats such as Portable Document Format (.pdf) by choosing **Download as** from the **File** menu.

Presentation

You can create presentations using Google Docs as an alternative to creating them using Microsoft Powerpoint, but don't (yet) expect to be able to do all of the things that PowerPoint allows you to do such as having complete control over the size and orientation of your slides. Also be aware that if you upload existing Powerpoint presentations to Google Docs, something may well be lost in the translation.

With the bad news out of the way, let me tell you the good news:

The idea of creating presentations "in the cloud" is a perfectly sound idea. Most presentations are created to be taken somewhere for showing, usually to another company. Some presenters have found themselves in the unfortunate position of having somehow lost, while traveling, the USB drive, DVD, or even laptop that contained the presentation. With your presentation in the cloud, you have no such worry. You can access it from your clients' computers in their offices or boardrooms with no possibility of losing anything in transit. As long as your client provides you with access to a web browser, that is.

When did you last attend a 'live' presentation anyhow? Haven't you noticed that many of the seminars that you would previously have attended in person have now been replaced with online 'webinars'? It makes sense if you want to reach an even wider international audience, and in this context the ability to embed a Google Docs presentation in a web page is one of the most useful features. Just choose **Publish to the web… / embed** from the **File** menu as shown here:

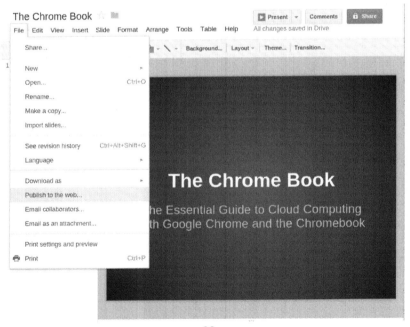

Once you have published the presentation to a unique web address URL for *all* to see (so beware) you can copy the embedding code that begins "**<iframe src=**" into your Blogger blog or other web site so as to embed the presentation as shown in this second example:

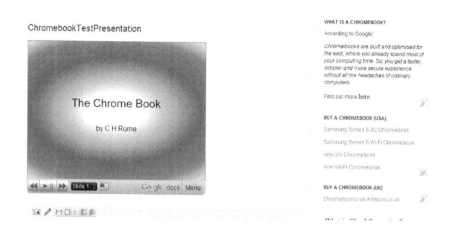

If you ever want to make the presentation unavailable, you can always click the **Stop publishing** button that is accessible via the **File / Publish to the web...** menu option.

Spreadsheet

Whereas the Google Docs 'Document' and 'Presentation' offerings can sometimes be a little restricting for my very exacting needs, I have found that the Spreadsheet offering more than lives up to what I would expect a spreadsheet program to do. It allows you to use formulas, functions, and cell references and retains most if not all of these when converting to and from Microsoft Excel (.xlsx) format.

The spreadsheet shown below is one that I created as an example that may be useful to financial traders who hope to re-enter a stock position at a lower price than the price at which they last sold; but the problem that this spreadsheet solves is not as important as the techniques it utilizes.

	Symbol	Price	Last Stop-Out	Want to...	Change Since Stop	%Change Since Stop	Open Signal	%Change Today	Info & Chart
3									
25	HAS.L	111.048	107.74	Long	3.31	3.07%		-1.64%	http://uk.financ
26	HDY.L	208.4	216	Long	-7.60	-3.52%	3.52%	-0.29%	http://uk.financ
27	HSD.L	157	160	Long	-3.00	-1.88%		-1.88%	http://uk.financ
28	INCH.L	377.8	299	Long	78.80	26.35%		1.27%	http://uk.financ
29	IFL.L	20	19	Long	1.00	5.26%		-3.60%	http://uk.financ
30	IPR.L	317.3	335	Long	-17.70	-5.28%	5.28%	-2.28%	http://uk.financ
31	IPO.L	49.5	29	Long	20.50	70.69%		3.13%	http://uk.financ
32	IPF.L	353.2	238	Long	115.20	48.40%		-3.42%	http://uk.financ
33	ITV.L	69.7	49	Long	20.70	42.24%		-1.48%	http://uk.financ
34	JJB.L	25	35	Long	-10.00	-28.57%	28.57%	-1.96%	http://uk.financ
35	JKX.L	288.7	285	Long	3.70	1.30%		-1.37%	http://uk.financ

In this spreadsheet the user is able to enter a **Stock Symbol** in the first column, and this cell entry is used to fetch live data from the World Wide Web using the following formula:

=ImportData("http://download.finance.yahoo.com/d/quotes.csv?f=sl 1d1t1c1ohgv&e=.csv&s="&$A26)

This is pretty powerful stuff, which replicates the Microsoft Excel capability for retrieving web data using a Web Query.

The live price retrieved into the second column is compared with the user-entered **Last Stop-Out** (i.e. last selling price) in the third column so as to calculate and color-code the **% Change** in the sixth column. This demonstrates the ability to apply conditional formatting to cell contents.

In the final **Info & Chart** column, the user-entered **Stock Symbol** has been formulated into a web address URL that links to the stock's chart on the Yahoo! Finance web site (sorry Google!) thus demonstrating the spreadsheet string manipulation functions.

This is just one example, and I have presented it to show that it really is possible to do with the Google Docs spreadsheet pretty much all of the things you would have done with Microsoft Excel. This includes the ability to produce charts from your data as illustrated below; and with

Google Docs you are able to publish your chart to a unique web address URL by clicking the **Publish chart** button that you can see in the picture.

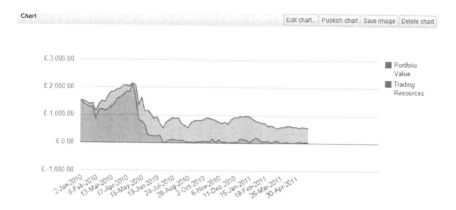

Form

You can use Google Docs to create a Form that you can embed in your website or blog to collect information from your visitors. The figure below shows a form that I created so that, in the run up to this book's release, my blog visitors could sign up to be notified as soon as the book became available. It's a simple form with only one text box for user input, but I can tell you that it is also possible to include pick lists and choice buttons in the forms you create.

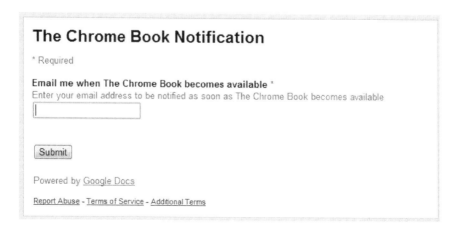

Each form that you create has a complementary spreadsheet, which is populated with a new entry each time a visitor submits your form; as illustrated below.

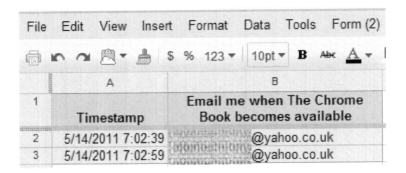

This basic form functionality will be most suited to those of you who want to add an element of interactivity to your website or blog without learning the necessary HTML code or other web programming techniques. One specific application for which I have found a Google Docs form to be most useful is in the provision of a web site 'contact me' form as an alternative to displaying an email address for all (including 'spammers') to see.

Drawing

As described in an earlier chapter, the chromebook has a basic image editor that allows you to manipulate a picture by cropping, changing the brightness, or rotating it. But what if you want to further manipulate the picture? Maybe you want to annotate it, or combine several such pictures into one. Maybe you want to create a brand new picture from scratch. In other words, you might want to do the things that you used to do with Microsoft Paint, which is where the Google Docs Drawing application comes in handy.

You can start a new drawing by choosing **Drawing** from the **Create new** pull-down menu in Google Docs, but I defer further discussion of the Drawing type to my case study chapter which provides a concrete example.

Sharing

Any Google Docs document, spreadsheet, presentation, or drawing can be shared with others by clicking the **Share** button at the top-right of the screen. You can also share any item within a collection / folder, or an entire collection / folder, by right-clicking the item in the Google Drive browser (not shown) and choosing the **Share** option. You should see the **Share settings** dialog, like this:

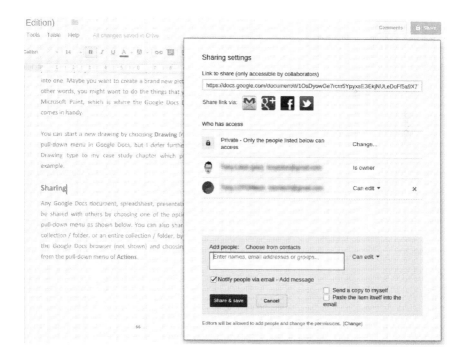

Sharing settings allow you to make an item **Private** so that only you and those people that you specify can access it (if they sign in to Google Docs). Alternatively, you can make an item available to **Anyone with the**

link (if you tell them the specific web address URL of the item) or you can make it **Public to the Web** so that it shows up in web searches. In all three cases you can decide whether those who have access can edit the item or merely view it.

Email editors/viewers...

Where you have entered a specific list of collaborators for a **Private item**, as shown above, you can **Notify people via email** with a message that also contains a link to the item.

Those people who you have deemed to be editors can post comments to your document as well as making changes to its content. Every posted comment is emailed to the document owner, and whenever the owner resolves a comment an email is sent to the editor who posted the comment. This can be both a blessing and a curse, as it can soon clog up your Inbox during an extensive reviewing and editing cycle.

Email as attachment...

In some cases you won't want to send out a hyperlink to the live item, but instead you will want to email a copy of the item as an attachment in a specific format like Microsoft Word (.docx) format. I would do this when submitting a written article to a magazine editor, by choosing the **Email as attachment** option from the document **File** menu.

It's exactly like emailing a document or other file as an attachment as you would usually do, but now you're attaching it straight from the cloud and emailing it using your Gmail email address. This is important because you are not using valuable bandwidth by downloading the file over the Internet to your own computer or chromebook simply to send it out again over the Internet.

Publish to the Web...

You can also choose to publish any Google Docs document to the web by choosing the **Publish to the web...** option from the document **File** menu.

A copy of the file will be published with a unique web address URL, and this copy can be refreshed (optionally) when changes are made to the original. Thus you might provide the general public with temporary access to a copy of your document without giving away the location of the original; and you can unpublish the copy whenever you like.

Google Docs Advantages

Now you have some idea of how Google Docs works and what you can do with it. But why would you want to use it? What does Google Docs give you that your PC office suite doesn't? Here are some suggestions:

- Your open documents are saved automatically at regular intervals, so you don't have to become obsessive-compulsive about pressing the CTRL-S keyboard combination every few minutes in case your PC crashes. Yes, I have suffered in the past from CTRL-S obsessive-compulsive disorder... and for very good reason.

- Your stored documents have a complete revision history. If you make a mistake, you can rollback to a previous version by choosing **See revision history** from the Google Docs **File** menu.

- Since your documents are stored online in the cloud (i.e. on a Google server computer) you can access them from any computer anywhere via a web browser.

- You can easily share your documents with viewers and collaborators without resorting to sending them as email attachments.

Here's the most compelling reason for making the move to Google Docs rather than upgrading to the next version of your PC office suite:

It's free! (at least for individuals)

Google Docs Disadvantages

The main disadvantage of using Google Docs is that to a large extent you have to be online to use it. You must be within range of a Wifi or 3G signal, you must be able to afford the data you are sending and receiving, and you are dependent on the performance of Google's server computers at the other end of your cloud connection. Personally, this is not a problem for me because most days I am connected to my 'all you can eat data' home / office broadband via Wifi. My fixed-line broadband deal grants me free access to thousands of FON Wifi hot spots (if I can find them!) while I'm out and about, and there are plenty of restaurants and bars that provide complimentary Wifi access to paying customers. If all else fails, I can get online via 3G as long as I can get a phone signal. Chapter *10 - Cloud Computing Conundrums* tells you how to do this via your Android phone.

Note that since the first edition of this book, it has become less essential for your chromebook to be connected to the Internet 100% of the time. You can create and edit Google Docs documents off-line, but at the time of writing this applies only to the Document file type and not the Spreadsheet which is view-only in offline mode.

The other disadvantage is that, for some people, the functionality is currently not quite up to the standard set by PC-based office packages like Microsoft Office and OpenOffice. For most of you, this won't be a problem, and it can cost you nothing to find out by taking Google Docs for a spin.

Alternatives to Google Docs

Since Chrome is merely a web browser running on your PC, chromebook or chromebox, you are not restricted to using Google Docs on your Google Drive as your online office suite.

For some time I was a fan of the Adobe Buzzword online word processor that never really caught on (and maybe no longer exists); and for something rather more mainstream you might try the Microsoft Office online apps – including online versions of Word and Excel – that are accessible via the Microsoft SkyDrive (which is more-or-less the Microsoft equivalent of the Google Drive).

Depending on your needs, you might also find some handy third party office apps in the Chrome Web Store. And I have some potentially exciting "office" news to share with you in the next chapter.

Chapter Summary

In this chapter I have described the various Google-format "office" files that you can create on your online Google Drive: Document, Presentation, Spreadsheet, Form and Drawing. I have introduced the idea of sharing your work and collaborating online, and I have rounded off by suggesting some advantages and disadvantages of these tools while also reminding you that there are alternatives.

In the next chapter we stay on the theme of "office" apps.

Find more **chromebook resources** including **books**, **chromebook computers** (if you don't already have one) and **compatible printers** at usa.thechromebook.info   or   uk.thechromebook.info.

---

8 – A Quick Look at QuickOffice

At the time of the Chromebook Pixel launch at the end of February 2013, Google also announced that they had updated the Chrome OS to include native (i.e. without converting to Google format) Microsoft Office viewing...with full editing capabilities to appear within three months.

Sure enough, it was possible to view Microsoft Word and Excel files locally without conversion at the time of the Chromebook Pixel launch (and not necessarily on a Chromebook Pixel model). And just over four months later, at the end of June 2013 I saw the first signs of these editing capabilities being made accessible via an obscure Chrome browser flag. I took the new Microsoft Office document and spreadsheet editing features for a brief spin on your behalf, and my initial findings are documented here... with the proviso that this is very early-stage stuff that may have changed somewhat by the time you read about it. Nevertheless, it should give you some food for thought regarding what is possible now and (more importantly) what may be possible in the future as a result of the Chrome / QuickOffice integration.

Going Native

In the context of this chapter, the phrase "going native" can be taken to mean two slightly different things:

1. Firstly, that the Chrome QuickOffice app(s) will allow you to edit Microsoft Office documents and spreadsheets in their native file formats without having to convert to the Google Docs file formats... and back again.
2. Secondly, I understand that the QuickOffice integration utilizes the Native Client functionality of the Chrome web browser that allows locally installed applications to access the computer hardware in ways that web-based apps cannot.

It's the first sense of the phrase "going native" that is most important, and the technicalities of how it is achieved is of lesser importance as long as the performance is adequate.

Enabling Document Editing

At the time of writing, you need to switch your chromebook onto the Chrome OS development channel as shown below. Note that switching to the Chrome OS development channel can cause the operation of your chromebook to become unstable, so for many of you it may be better to wait until this goes mainstream on the stable channel.

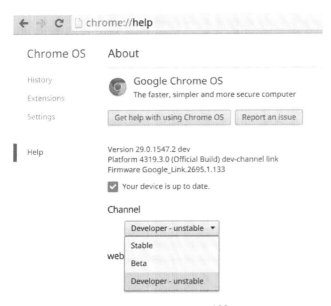

Next you need to enable the **chrome://flags/#enable-quickoffice-editing** flag (see second picture below).

Editing Word Documents

Once document editing had been enabled, opening a Microsoft Office document for editing was simply a matter of clicking the compatible document (Word or Excel file) and pressing the Chrome Office Viewer button (which may be labeled differently by the time you read this):

Whereas Office documents would previously have been displayed in "view" mode, the **#enable-quickoffice-editing** flag now causes the document to open in the editing mode of the QuickOffice browser-based application. At first glance, this looks promising—with the document presented nicely enough, and with any keyboard key presses being reflected in the document text. See here:

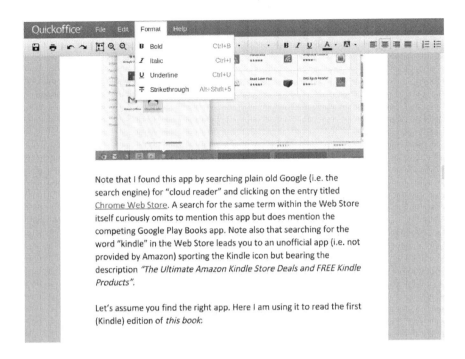

Note that I found this app by searching plain old Google (i.e. the search engine) for "cloud reader" and clicking on the entry titled Chrome Web Store. A search for the same term within the Web Store itself curiously omits to mention this app but does mention the competing Google Play Books app. Note also that searching for the word "kindle" in the Web Store leads you to an unofficial app (i.e. not provided by Amazon) sporting the Kindle icon but bearing the description *"The Ultimate Amazon Kindle Store Deals and FREE Kindle Products"*.

Let's assume you find the right app. Here I am using it to read the first (Kindle) edition of *this book*:

Further investigation reveals the shortcomings, which at the time of writing include (but are not limited to):

- Document images appear to be stretched vertically, and there are apparently no facilities for inserting or editing images.
- Page headers and footers are not visible, let alone editable.
- Paging is not as in the original Word document.
- Response to key presses is slooooow, with a very noticeable lag even on my top-of-the-range Chromebook Pixel.
- The QuickOffice application crashed on me while attempting to edit the Word document, and it appeared that my work had not been auto-saved—this auto-saving being one of the really nice features of the alternative Google Docs online word processor.

Editing Excel Spreadsheets

My experience with the experimental edition of the QuickOffice Excel editor was similar to my experience with the Word editor. At first glance, it seemed to load up an Excel spreadsheet just fine and to allow editing of the cells' contents:

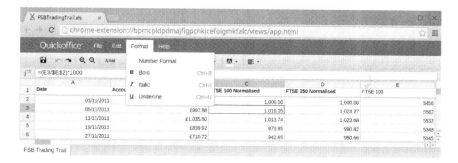

On closer inspection there remained a lot to be desired. Inexplicably, the chart for the pictured spreadsheet failed to display. Another spreadsheet caused the editor to crash. And as you can see from my screenshot, the menu options – including the one to Format cells – were (at the time of writing) sparsely populated.

The Verdict

I don't want to be too harsh here, because – at the time of writing – this is still very experimental Chrome software. But four months after the announcement that "full editing capabilities" would be available within three months, I have to admit to feeling somewhat disappointed. In particular, I had been hoping to write the entire manuscript for the fourth edition of this book entirely using Chrome QuickOffice—just as I had substantially written previous editions using the Google Docs word processor.

At this point I'm philosophical that the integrated QuickOffice apps present us with a glimpse of what is to come. It is certainly possible (just about) to open Word and Excel files on a chromebook without converting to Google Drive format, and to perform limited editing functions. And on the issue of "limited editing" it is worth drawing a comparison with Microsoft's own Office web apps.

In case you didn't know, it is perfectly possible to create brand new Word documents and Excel spreadsheets, and edit existing ones, via the Chrome web browser on a chromebook or any other device, by taking advantage of the Microsoft Office web apps at www.skydrive.com. Right now, it's probably the best way to do it. But these too are not fully functional Office apps because, while they preserve the integrity of the original files, they allow only limited edits to be performed. For example, it is not currently possible to add page breaks to a Word document using the Microsoft Word web app, but any existing page breaks in a preexisting document are preserved throughout the editing process. It looks to me like the Chrome QuickOffice apps are destined to function in a similar way: to preserve the integrity of the original documents while supporting a limited (but growing) set of possible edits. We'll see.

Find more **chromebook resources** including **books**, **chromebook computers** (if you don't already have one) and **compatible printers** at usa.thechromebook.info or uk.thechromebook.info.

---

9 - Google Apps for Your Business

The greater part of this book is focused on the single user or family member who has bought a chromebook and has signed up for a Google account for personal use. This is only part of the chromebook story, because Google is also inroads into the corporate market with chromebooks. It makes sense because, while notionally expensive for mere web browsing devices, chromebooks offer potentially a lower "total cost of ownership" for a business. This is because it is very difficult if not impossible for individual users to install software programs – and inadvertently, viruses – onto the machines. In any case, many businesses require their employees to use a limited "locked down" set of software programs that are often served up via the company intranet; think about travel agencies, car rental firms, bank staff, and public libraries. In the latter case, the ability for anyone to browse the web using a chromebook as a "guest" makes these devices ideal for public internet access in libraries.

Corporate clients will likely be interested in providing their staff with chromebooks complemented by the more commercially-oriented Google Apps accounts; and that is the subject of this chapter. It's a relatively short (and optional) chapter because this book is still mainly about Google's Chromebook, Chrome web browser and cloud computing ecosystem as seen from the retail consumers' perspective.

A Brief History of Thin-Client Computing

Why equip every one of your employees with an overpowered and overpriced PC or Mac when most if not all of their tasks involve interacting with web applications provided via the Internet or via your company intranet? Wouldn't a simpler desktop or in-the-field terminal – rather like the old mainframe "green screen" terminals, but now in full Technicolor – be more appropriate? And just think about how much money you could save by not employing armies of technical staff to keep all of those traditional PCs and Macs up-to-date and virus free.

It's been done before with mainframe computing. It's been tried before with the never-widely-adopted Sun Microsystems 'JavaStation' terminals that aimed to reduce total cost of ownership (TCO) to near zero. But what makes it truly possible this time around is the ubiquity of broadband Internet access.

In fact, your company may already be doing cloud computing. Using technologies like Citrix, many companies have for some time been allowing their staff to run office applications like Microsoft Word on their remotely-connected laptop or desktop PCs without actually having the Microsoft Office suite installed on those machines. The software runs on the server computers back at base, and any field computer merely provides a window on the remote computing session. This kind of corporate cloud computing lessens the burden of installing and configuring the software individually on numerous client computers, and it fits neatly with the chromebook philosophy of having no software – well, not much of it – installed locally on the user's device.

I bet you've heard numerous scandal stories about government, military, and commercial laptops containing sensitive data having been left on trains. With chromebooks there is less danger, because you should lose only the laptop and not the sensitive information it contains. The idea is that hardly anything is stored locally, and anything that is – including temporary Internet files – is encrypted.

In terms of enabling the worldwide workforce, Google initially instigated *Chromebooks for Business* and *Chromebooks for Education* programs to 'rent' chromebooks to businesses and educational establishments for between $20 (education) and $28 (business) per month. When you consider that this would have made the $429 Samsung Series 5 chromebook cost twice as much over the 36-month minimum term it sounded expensive; but when you considered that you could dramatically cut your IT support costs, and effectively outsource the rest to Google for the all-inclusive price, it began to sound much more reasonable.

Companies that originally piloted the use of chromebooks in their organizations included American Airlines, Intercontinental Hotels Group, Groupon, Logitech, Konica Minolta, National Geographic, and Virgin America.

So, Who Needs Google Apps?

Some companies will have adopted the Google cloud computing model by signing up with Google Apps and (optionally) by equipping their staff with easy-maintenance chromebooks as an alternative to high-maintenance PCs. It may be via this route that you got your chromebook and / or started using Google's web-based alternatives to the software programs you were used to. Or it may be that you have your own small business and you want to equip your staff with email addresses, communal calendar facilities, basic office functions, and simple devices (i.e. chromebooks) to access those facilities without the need for an expensive and expansive IT department overhead.

Signing Up for Google Apps

There are at least two ways that I know of for signing up with Google Apps for your commercial enterprise:

1. Visit the web page at **apps.google.com** and **Start Free Trial** (if it's still available).

2. Apply for a Google-supplied custom domain for your Blogger blog (see screenshot below) and get Google Apps thrown in for your new domain.

What You Get with Google Apps

Google Apps allows you as a business owner to provide your staff with a complete set of office tools through which they can collaborate online. The current lineup of tools includes Gmail, Calendar, Drive (incorporating Docs, Sheets, and Slides), Sites (which is rather like Microsoft SharePoint as far as I can tell), and Vault (for audited archiving).

Note that the emphasis is on online storage (so that all data is automatically backed up) and collaboration (so that users can easily arrange meetings and work on the same documents at the same time).

Managing Multiple Users

Suppose you signed up with Google Apps as a new company called LOTONtech Limited. Well, obviously *you* might not want to do this, but of course *I* would. And if I did, I would likely create a new user account for the pseudo-named author of this book (C H Rome) as shown below.

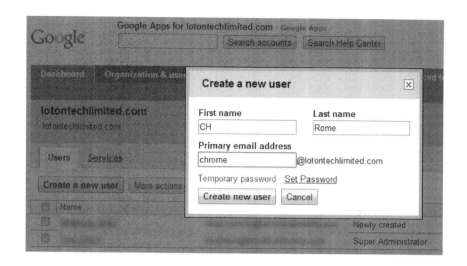

This new user could henceforth sign in to a chromebook or chromebox, or a PC running the Chrome web browser, using the email address that was allocated. He could also sign in via another web browser using this company-specific web address:

http://www.google.com/a/lotontechlimited.com
(don't go there, it's not worth it)

Although each user's experience of Gmail, Google Drive and so on would be pretty much the same as the individual user experience described throughout this book, I (as the business owner) would be able to manage these users by assigning them specific privileges and allocating them to groups.

Chapter Summary

I told you that this chapter would be short and sweet, and I've been true to my word. The purpose has been merely to highlight the fact that even a modest enterprise can establish a multi-user enterprise-wide IT infrastructure ... without the IT infrastructure. All thanks to cloud computing with Google Apps.

Find more **chromebook resources** including **books**, **chromebook computers** (if you don't already have one) and **compatible printers** at usa.thechromebook.info or uk.thechromebook.info.

10 - Cloud Computing Conundrums

The low-maintenance chromebook and chromebox computers, and the wider Google cloud computing model, present a set of conundrums in the form of tasks that you used to be able to perform quite easily using your traditional PC, but which the cloud computing model makes more difficult. In this chapter I present some of those cloud computing conundrums, and (most helpfully) the potential solutions.

But first, let me start by stating that the Chrome OS doesn't at all present one of the conundrums presented by the comparative Apple devices such as the iPad. Many of the financial trading web sites and other web sites that I use daily require my computing device (laptop, phone or tablet) to run Adobe Flash content in the web browser. On the iPad and on other Apple iOS powered devices this is simply impossible, because those devices won't run Flash. The chromebooks and chromeboxes have no such limitation, and they run Flash web sites just fine.

Okay, so much for what Chrome OS devices can do that the iPad can't. Now what about those things that chromebooks, chromeboxes and other Chrome OS devices struggle with?

Printing

The most obvious cloud computing problem is printing. Chromebooks were designed not to run locally-installed software, and this includes printer drivers, so there is little point trying to attach a printer directly to your chromebook computer. If you try to do so, your chromebook should at least present a web page inviting you to **Add Classic printer** or **Add Cloud Ready printer**, so at least it recognizes the fact that attaching a printer is what you tried to do.

The "paperless office" has been a little slower in materializing than we might have hoped, and therefore most of us still need to print content as hard copy (i.e. on paper) from time to time. The printing conundrum can be addressed in a number of ways as follows.

Since the printing problem is not only a problem for users of chromebooks and chromeboxes, but also a problem for users of smart phones and tablets that don't generally allow you to attach printers directly, Hewlett Packard came up with an ingenious solution in the form of its ePrint range of printers.

These printers connect up to HP's ePrint service on the Internet via your wireless router, and allow you to associate an email address with the printer. Printing on one of these printers from your chromebook, phone or tablet – even from miles away – can be as simple as sending your document as an email attachment to:

emailaddressofmyprinter@hpeprint.com *(not a real email address)*

If the email address of your printer became widely known, anyone could print to it, although it's anyone's guess as to why they would want to. To inundate you with hard copy SPAM advertisements, I guess.

Rest assured that it is possible to configure the settings via the ePrint Center web site at https://h30495.www3.hp.com/ so that only recognized email addresses (the **Allowed Senders**) can send print jobs to your printer.

Check the range of HP ePrint printer-scanners at:

usa.thechromebook.info

uk.thechromebook.info

Google Cloud Print

On the HP ePrint Settings dialog just shown, you can see a third tab labeled **Print Services**, and here lies the second solution to the printing conundrum – in the form of Google Cloud Print.

Once you've registered a printer with the Google Cloud Print Service – which means associating it with your Google account – you can print to it as though the printer is attached to your chromebook or chromebox. You can see the **Google Cloud Print** dialog in the following screenshot, via which I have chosen to send a document from Gmail running on my chromebook to a HP Photosmart printer that I had previously registered with Google Cloud Print.

Note that alternatively you can **Save as PDF**, which enables you to store a "printed" copy of your content (in this case an email message) as an electronic Portable Document Format (PDF) file in your chromebook's **Downloads** folder – from where you might copy it to your **Google Drive** for permanent safekeeping.

Note also that your connected printer need not be a HP printer, it might be a Canon or some other printer brand, and it need not be an e-printer at all... as I will now explain.

Connecting Your PC Printer to Google Cloud Print

When running the Chrome web browser on your traditional PC, the browser **Settings** (as shown below) should include a section titled **Google Cloud Print**. In the case of my screenshot below, I already have some printers connected, therefore I can **Disconnect printers**, but you should not have this option... yet.

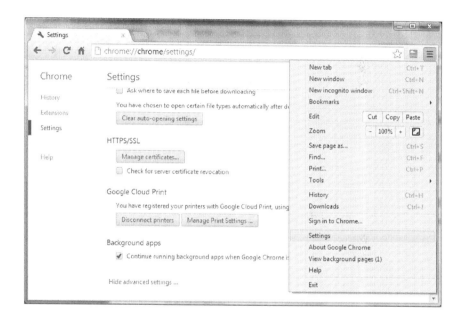

If you never did this before, you will have the option to **Add Printers**, and after signing into your Google account you should find that any printer attached to your PC will be registered with the Cloud Print Service. It means that as long as your PC is switched on and connected to the Internet, you can print to its attached printer(s) from your chromebook or chromebox via Cloud Print. This is a useful interim solution for those people who continue to own legacy PC hardware (and printers) while transitioning to the world of cloud computing with Chrome.

Scanning Documents

The opposite of *printing a document from a computer* is *scanning a document to a computer*. Again, this task is not so obviously easy to perform using a chromebook that does not allow you to install your scanner's driver software. But all is not lost, because (in my case) my HP ePrint printer-scanner offers two possible solutions.

The first solution could not be simpler. Just pop an SD card into the slot on the printer-scanner, choose the option on the printer display panel to scan to Memory Card, and then pop the SD card into the side of my Chromebook (Pixel).

The second solution is almost as easy. Find the printer's Wireless settings on the printer-scanner display panel and note down the printer's IP address: let's say it is 123.456.7.89, which of course is not the real address.

Upon typing the printer-scanner's IP address into the Chrome web browser's address bar, I am presented with the printer's web page that includes an option to **Scan to Computer using Webscan**. Here is a picture showing how I successfully scanned the cover of the third edition of this book:

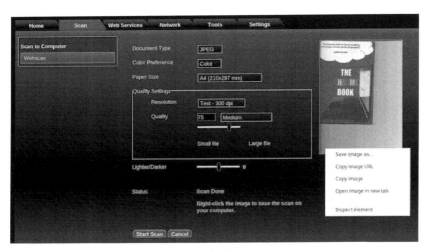

I have to say that this didn't go 100% smoothly the first time around, because I had to enable the Webscan function in the **Settings** tab (see the picture), and then I had to restart the printer otherwise the scanned image seemed to be blank when trying to **Save image as...** on my chromebook. But all's well that ends well, and it did end well for me.

Depending on your make and model of scanner or printer-scanner, you may not be able to scan documents in exactly the way I have described, but I hope my description gives you hope that this important task is at least possible one way or another when using a suitable printer.

Once again, you can check the range of HP ePrint printer-scanners at:

usa.thechromebook.info

uk.thechromebook.info

Using an External Display

One topic that didn't find its way into the third edition of this book is the topic of attaching an external display such as a television screen to your chromebook. So now I plug that gap.

The first thing you'll need is a suitable cable, and since I'm using the Chromebook Pixel (USA or UK) as my demonstration vehicle, the cable I need is a Mini Display Port to HDMI (USA or UK) cable. Your chromebook might sport a standard HDMI port that takes a regular HDMI cable or a mini HDMI cable.

The next step is to connect up the chromebook to the TV using the cable, and to select the required input source (i.e. HDMI) on the TV. In the following picture you can see how I have my Chromebook Pixel and attached TV configured so that I'm using the Pixlr Image Editor web app on the chromebook screen... while watching a YouTube video about lions on the "big screen" TV.

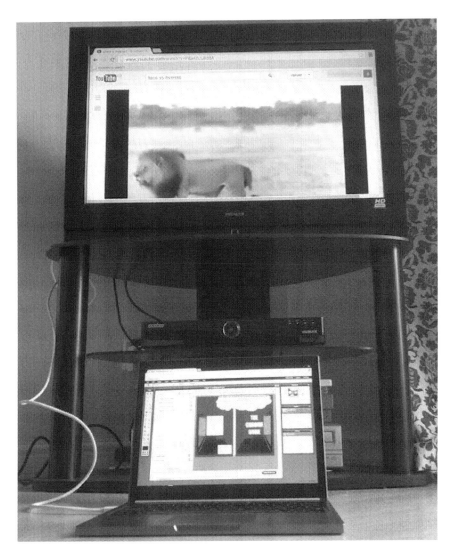

By default the TV screen extends your chromebook screen to the right, so my objective was achieved simply by dragging the YouTube browser window all the way to the right – off the chromebook screen and onto the TV screen – and then maximizing it.

The alternative is to mirror the content of the chromebook screen on the attached screen, which can be done simply by pressing **ctrl +**

on the chromebook keyboard. Press it again to toggle back to the extended display mode.

You will be interested to know that you can also **Manage displays** via the dialog shown below, which is accessible (in my case) by selecting the **Extending screen to 32_LCD_TV** item from the status panel (bottom right) as shown below.

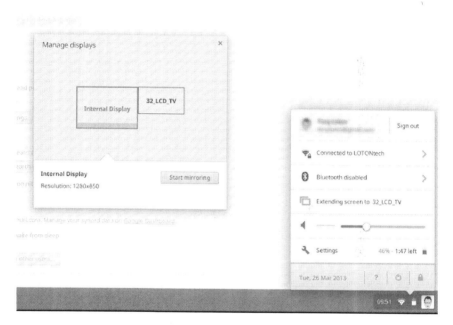

Windows Programs via the Chrome Remote Desktop

I reckon I can exist 90% "in the cloud", simply interacting with Google Apps and the other websites I use on a regular basis. But as a book publisher I also do some pretty hardcore stuff using Microsoft Word.

Reconciling these two worlds – my desire to carry only a chromebook with me wherever I go, and my need to access the advanced features of Microsoft Word – presents me with a problem. Or does it?

I have a perfectly serviceable desktop PC that runs Microsoft Word, and I have a broadband router that allows this desktop PC to be always connected to the Internet. If only there was a way to somehow "dial in" to this PC from my chromebook, and to interact with it via the chromebook keyboard and screen (from wherever I happen to be at the time), then I wouldn't be limited by the fact that I can't run this Windows software directly on my chromebook.

You won't be surprised to learn that I'm leading up to the fact that... you can do exactly what I just described, by using the Chrome Remote Desktop. Here's how...

On Your PC

First you need to do a little setup at the PC end.

Using the Chrome web browser, visit the Web Store at https://chrome.google.com/webstore and search for "chrome remote desktop". When you find the **Chrome Remote Desktop** app, click the button marked **ADD TO CHROME**, followed by the button to **LAUNCH APP**.

You will be prompted to select a Google account, and then to **Allow Access**.

The remote desktop has a **Remote Assistance** option which is intended for technical support staff to gain temporary access to someone else's computer, and a **My Computers** option that allows you to access and operate your home or office-based PC remotely from your chromebook.

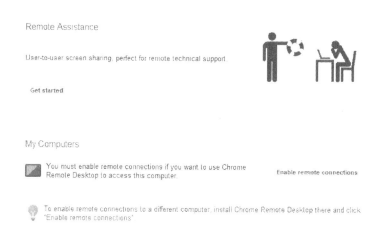

Upon clicking the **Enable remote connections** button shown in the screenshot above, you will be prompted to enter a PIN that ensures only you can access your PC remotely. Once the remote desktop feature has been enabled, you should ensure that the PC (especially if a laptop) power settings are such that it will not go to sleep just when you really want to access it remotely.

On Your Chromebook

Once you've set up the PC end of the remote connection you can launch the Chrome Remote Desktop app on your chromebook. You should see your PC listed in the **My Computers** section of the page as shown below, and you can simply click (and enter your PIN) to connect.

Everything you do on your PC screen will appear automatically on your chromebook screen, and vice versa, which can be quite spooky. You can operate your PC from your chromebook *as though it is your PC*, and can run all your favorite programs... even if you're in another room or another city. The following screenshot shows my Chrome Remote Desktop session running Microsoft Word.

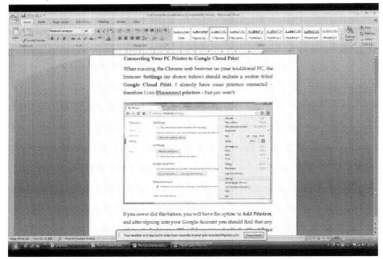

Here's a tip: it looks much better if you go full-screen in the Chrome browser so that your screen is filled with the contents of the PC screen. If you have another Chrome browser window running on your chromebook, perhaps for your Gmail, you can easily switch between the "PC screen" and chromebook screen(s) by pressing the "switch windows" key on the chromebook keyboard.

With the Chrome Remote Desktop running in full-screen mode on the Chromebook Pixel's high resolution screen, it really is as though your chromebook is a Windows laptop. This brings me to...

The Chromebook as a Windows 8 Ultrabook

Don't get too excited, I'm not about to tell you how you can install Windows 8 on your chromebook. But I was interested to know what would happen if I connected up to a Windows 8 PC from a touch screen Chromebook Pixel via the Chrome Remote Desktop app; i.e. whether the Chromebook Pixel touch screen could be used to drive the Windows 8 touch interface.

Let's start with a picture of the Chromebook Pixel connected up to a Windows 8 PC via the Chrome Remote Desktop:

With the Chrome Remote Desktop running in full screen mode, this is a neat way of convincing onlookers that you're operating one of the latest smartest-looking Windows 8 ultrabooks rather than a chromebook.

Now I'll tell you what I found to work (and not), although I admit that my findings could be affected by the fact that I was running a Windows 8 "preview" installation on a PC that didn't itself have a touch screen capability:

- Tiles on the Windows 8 Start screen could be selected by tapping them on the Chromebook Pixel touch screen, and could be moved around by tapping and holding.
- The Start screen could not be panned left and right by swiping left and right on the Chromebook Pixel touch screen, but placing two fingers side-by-side on the touch pad and moving them up and down achieved the desired effect. Strange, but true!
- Swiping from just off the right and bottom edges of the screen didn't seem to work, so I had to resort to moving the mouse cursor to the bottom left and right corners of the screen in order to reveal the Windows 8 Start icon and the Charms bar.
- When using the Windows 8 Maps app, pinch-and-zoom on the Chromebook Pixel touch screen didn't work, but sliding two fingers up and down the touch pad had the desired effect for zooming in and out on the map. The maps could be moved around the screen, as expected, by placing one finger on the touch screen and moving it around.

This was only a cursory experiment with a non-ideal setup, but which nonetheless convinced me that there is some value in operating a Windows 8 PC via the Chrome Remote Desktop app using the Chromebook Pixel touch screen.

Internet Connection via 3G on Your Mobile Phone

Some people prefer the convenience of a 3G-enabled chromebook on which they can obtain an essential Internet connection wherever they can get a mobile signal; although a Wifi connection would almost always be more cost-effective where available.

Some people are happy enough to opt for a cheaper Wifi-only chromebook model and to rely solely on Wifi hotspots at home, at work, or in public places (like restaurants) for the essential Internet connection.

I'm in the latter camp because if I really need to connect my chromebook to the Internet via 3G, I can do so using my Android mobile phone. It saves me from having separate mobile data contracts for my phone and my chromebook, and – theoretically, at least – it means I can connect my chromebook via the much-faster 4G mobile network in future by simply upgrading my phone and without having to upgrade my chromebook.

I can connect my non-3G chromebook to the Internet via 3G by enabling my Android phone for USB Tethering or as a Portable Wifi Hotspot. For the record, the phone I am using to achieve this feat is a two-and-a-half year old Google / Samsung Nexus S phone running Android version 4.1.2 (it also worked on some earlier versions) and connected to the UK's "3" mobile 3G network. You may or may not be able to achieve the same thing as me, depending on your phone and mobile carrier.

Tethering & portable hotspot

Within the **WIRELESS & NETWORKS** section of your Android phone's **Settings**, you should see an option labeled **Tethering and portable hotspot**. Selecting this option should present you with a number of options as shown in the following screenshot; options for **USB Tethering**, **Portable Wi-Fi hotspot**, and **Bluetooth tethering**.

The most straightforward option is the **USB tethering** option which will be grayed-out unless you have connected your phone to your chromebook using a USB cable. Once you've connected the cable and enabled the option, you should see a new network named **Ethernet** on your chromebook:

In the list of networks shown above, you can also see a network named **LOTONtech3**, which is a wireless network that became available when I enabled the **Portable Wi-Fi hotspot option** on my Android phone.

The final option is to tether your Android phone and your chromebook together using the **Bluetooth tethering** option, but I'll leave that one for you to try yourself. I've never been a big fan of the additional "pairing" step that is required in order to get Bluetooth devices to play together.

Chapter Summary

The Chrome cloud computing model presents some interesting opportunities to work and play in ways that were simply not possible before; but it also presents some challenges such as how to print and how to run the (Windows) software programs that you used to know and love. So in the chapter I have addressed some of those cloud computing conundrums. For many of you, this will have been the most useful chapter of the book.

When it comes to one of the solutions in particular – the Chrome Remote Desktop – I personally use this feature rather more than I expected; for example when sitting on my bed (chromebook on my lap) while the remotely-connected PC that I am interacting with is sitting in my office.

Find more **chromebook resources** including **books, chromebook computers** (if you don't already have one) and **compatible printers** at usa.thechromebook.info or uk.thechromebook.info.

---

11 - Cloud Computing Case Study

It's all very well me telling you how you can now do almost everything via web apps in the cloud, but it's time for me to put my money where my mouth is by demonstrating how I can run my own business in the cloud... by creating and publishing the book you are reading now using (wherever possible) only cloud-based tools. My publishing business has certain cloud-unfriendly characteristics that necessitate certain compromises, but if I can run my business in the cloud (just about) then so can you.

I know that your business is unlikely to be a publishing business, but many of the business tasks covered by this case study – like creating documents, creating a web site and doing some basic e-commerce – will be applicable to many different businesses. Many of the technical tasks – like word processing and manipulating images – will be applicable to many business and personal computing scenarios.

Don't take these steps as verbatim instructions for creating the optimal publish-quality book. My intention is merely to demonstrate that with a little ingenuity and lateral thinking, it could be possible (at least in theory) for you to transition from PC-based software to cloud-based web tools; even if not these specific tools.

The Google Document (for the book content)

The first thing I need to do in my endeavor to publish a book is to actually write the manuscript for the book's content, which I have done in this case in the form of a Google Document. Before I begin writing the words, I need to first set the page size and margins.

Page setup

I intended to publish this book ultimately with my usual book trim size (page size) of 6" x 9" (15.24cm x 22.86cm), but unfortunately this page size is not supported for a Google Document so I opted for the nearest size of 14.0cm x 21.6cm as shown below. It corresponds almost exactly with the CreateSpace publishing platform's 5.5" x 8.5" trim size.

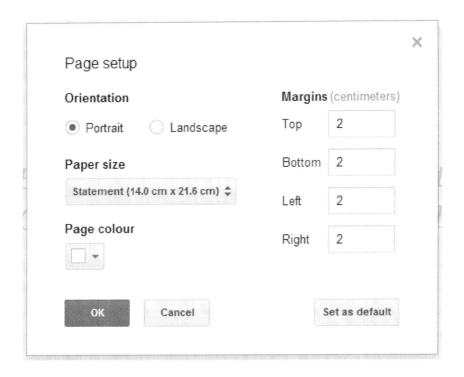

Ideally a printed book would have an internal "gutter" of extra space on the inside edges of pages for binding. This "mirror margins" feature is not supported for a Google Document, so I have opted for 2cm margins all round.

Styles

When writing any document using any word processor it is important to apply the built-in styles for **Normal text** and for headings such as **Heading 1** and **Heading 2**. You can re-style these built-in styles by changing the font, font size, and characteristics (such as bold) and then right-clicking your selected text in order to access the context menu with the option to (in this case) **Update 'Heading 3' to match**. Selecting appropriate fonts and sizes for the various styles will make your document look more professional—especially if it is destined for print.

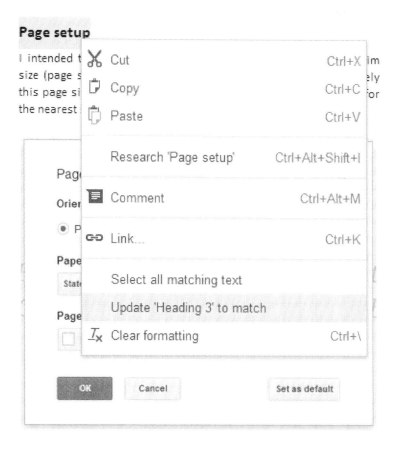

Headers and Footers

While it is perfectly possible to insert headers and footers onto the pages of a Google Document, it is not obvious (if at all possible) how to prevent those headers and footers from appearing on every single page. This is a problem when creating a printed book or report for which you do not wish the header to appear atop the title page or any new chapter page. In the absence of a "first page header" feature, I have opted not to use headers but to use simple footers displaying merely the page number. This can be achieved simply by choosing **Page number /** **Bottom of page** from the **Insert** menu.

Images

This book contains many screenshots which I captured by pressing the **ctrl + switch windows** ( ) key combination. I cropped those images using the Files app, or otherwise edited them using the more feature-rich Pixlr app. Finally, I inserted the images by selecting the **Image** option from the Google Document **Insert** menu. I prefer to place images in line with text, but it is also possible to place images at a fixed page position by right-clicking as shown in this picture:

Clicking the small cog wheel at the top-right of your Gmail screen initiates a p select the option to In line with text | Fixed position

Peer Review and Editing

Every author should want their manuscript to be peer reviewed, edited, or simply proofread by someone else. I wanted my assistant to proofread this book, so I simply shared the Google Document with her by clicking the **Share** button and typing my invitation as shown below.

Add people: Choose from contacts

▭▭▭▭▭ ▭▭▭▭▭▭▭▭▭▭▭   Can edit ▾

☑ Notify people via email - Discard message

Hi Becky, could you please proofread this book manuscript as usual?

Thanks!

Share & save   Cancel

☐ Send a copy to myself
☐ Paste the item itself into the
email

By marking Becky as someone who **Can edit** the document, I am allowing her to insert comments and text changes directly in the document without us having to email a copy of the manuscript back and forth.

From Content to Cover

With the book's content having now been written, styled, and edited / reviewed as a Google Document, it is now time to use another Google tool to design the book cover.

The Google Drawing (for the book front cover)

Every book needs a book cover, and creating the cover for my book affords me the opportunity to demonstrate one of the other Google Drive document types: the Google Drawing.

When you first create a drawing you will be presented with a canvas of a default size, and with no obvious way of changing the canvas size apart from dragging the right-hand corner downwards and to the right. Since you can't drag any further than your chromebook screen will allow, you may first need to zoom out before dragging to the required canvas size.

I already know that my chosen CreateSpace book trim size will require me to upload a front cover image measuring a slightly larger 5.75" x 9" at ideally 300 DPI (dots-per-inch), which in a nutshell means an image of 1725 x 2700 pixels. At the time of writing, it is only possible to create a Google Drawing with a maximum size of 2000 x 2000 pixels, which therefore obliges me to compromise on a size of 1278 x 2000 pixels for my required aspect ratio. This will mean a lower-than-optimal 222 DPI (dots per inch) – but hey, I said there would be compromises!

Actually, you don't have to compromise at all, because there are other web apps and websites (like Pixlr) that allow the creation and manipulation of images, but my objective here is to stick with the Google-originated tools as far as possible.

To continue my story: I created a blank drawing in the required size, and immediately saved it under the name **BookCoverTemplate** before choosing to **Make a copy** (from the **File** menu) for the actual cover design.

I already quite liked the design that I had created for the *second edition* cover of this book, so I decided to replicate it by uploading a side-on perspective photograph of an actual chromebook (in this case the Chromebook Pixel) to be positioned hard up against the lower-right corner of the front cover. In summary, I was able to begin creating a front cover design with the Drawing tool that looked something like this:

Note that at the time of writing, any images you upload to a Drawing must be less than 2mb in size.

One good thing about the Google Drawing tool is that all of the photographs, text boxes and other graphical elements that you place are at all times individually selectable rather than being "baked into" the final image as they would be when using Pixlr. So you can move, resize, and otherwise arrange them to your heart's content when using a Google Drawing.

From Content and Cover to CreateSpace

I now have the content and a cover for my book, and so it is time to upload those creations to the CreateSpace publishing platform.

Publishing as a Print Book via CreateSpace

This book was published in paperback form using Amazon's CreateSpace self-publishing platform at www.createspace.com. It's entirely web-based, and – although the devil is in the detail – publishing via this route can be as simple as downloading the Google Document in PDF (or another format), downloading the Google Drawing as a JPG, and uploading both to the CreateSpace publishing platform.

Downloading and Uploading the Book Interior

Historically, I have always found it best to export in Portable Document Format (PDF) from the source word processor and to upload this "print ready" PDF file to CreateSpace for publishing; but I have found that exporting a Google Document in PDF format can result in significantly degraded image quality. The best solution to this problem appears to be to "print" the Document to a PDF file like this:

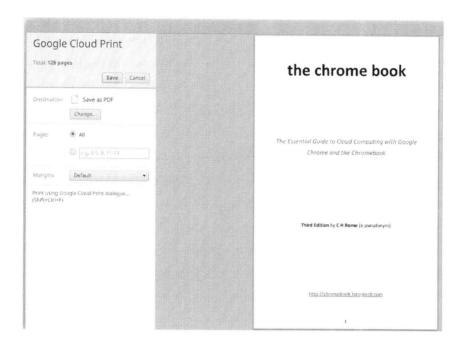

You can export a Google Document in other formats that are acceptable to CreateSpace, such as Rich Text Format (.rtf) and Microsoft Word (.docx). RTF seems to convert best on CreateSpace but I have encountered problems downloading a Google Document in RTF format once it reaches a certain size. Google Documents always seem to download fine in Microsoft Word (.docx) format– unless they contain unresolved "comments", in which case the file might be reported by Microsoft Word as corrupt. I would usually export in this format with a view to "finishing" the manuscript preparation using the bona fide Microsoft Word.

As you will no doubt have concluded, there are some issues to be resolved when using a Google Document as the source of a CreateSpace print-on-demand book, but these are no more taxing than the problems I personally encountered originally when trying to use Microsoft Word for the same purpose. Every new way of working involves a learning curve, and having worked around the aforementioned problems, the following screenshot shows what my book manuscript looked like when uploaded to the CreateSpace website and previewed using the reviewing tool. It's beginning to look like a proper book, isn't it?

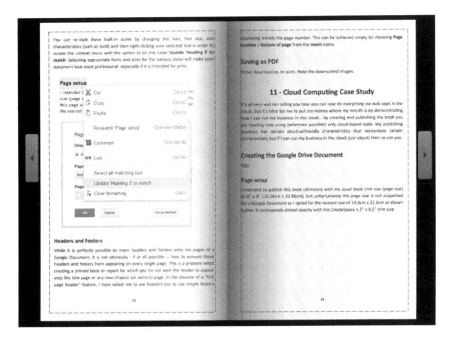

Finishing Touches with Microsoft Word

Although it is "just about" possible to create a book manuscript fully "in the cloud" as a Google Document, if you have access to Microsoft Word at home or at work you might want to open the Microsoft Word (.docx) file that you downloaded from the Google Document and use the bona fide Microsoft Word to apply some final professional touches: like adding an index and (possibly) generating the final print-ready PDF to be uploaded to CreateSpace. But you can get by without it.

Downloading and Uploading the Book Cover

For this case study, my ideal would have been to export my Google Drawing cover design in JPG format – choose **File / Download as / JPEG image (.jpg)** – which is one of the formats acceptable to CreateSpace. I have found that this results in a lower quality image compared with if I save the Drawing in **PNG image (.png)** format and then use a PC program or web app to convert to the CreateSpace-acceptable JPG format. Again, we have to compromise or find new ways of doing things when transitioning to cloud computing.

Once I was able to download the front cover design in an acceptable format at a (just about) acceptable level of quality, I was able to upload to the CreateSpace two-piece book cover design template as shown below.

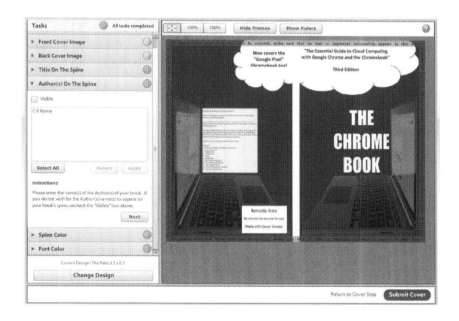

Additional steps are required to fully publish a book via CreateSpace, but those details don't belong here. Right now it is sufficient for me to say that the proof of the pudding is in the publishing, and if you're reading this then you must have seen the results of my efforts detailed above. Or maybe you're witnessing the results of my...

Publishing as a Kindle e-Book

This book was published in e-book form using Amazon's Kindle Direct Publishing (KDP) platform at kdp.amazon.com. It's entirely web-based, and publishing via this route can be as simple as downloading the Google Document in Microsoft Word (.docx) format, downloading the Google Drawing as a JPG, and uploading both to the KDP publishing platform.

Bookmarks and Links

One difference between e-books and print books is that e-books can contain hyperlinks to external web sites and to sections within the book. It is common to navigate an e-book by clicking a hyperlinked *Table of Contents* rather than by relying on page numbers (which may in fact be meaningless in a free flowing e-book).

In the following picture you can see how I am linking a *Table of Contents* entry (select **Insert / Link** in the Google Document) to a bookmark that I had previously placed in the document at the first chapter (by selecting **Insert / Bookmark**).

I should tell you that documents destined for uploading to the KDP platform can also be adorned with bookmarks denoting the location of the *Table of Contents* (bookmark name "TOC") and the beginning of the e-book (bookmark name "Start"). This is easier said than done in a Google Document compared with Microsoft Word, because there appears to be no way to specify a bookmark name except by highlighting text to be bookmarked, but it's not a showstopper.

Publishing Direct

As well as publishing my book on Amazon in print and Kindle formats, I'd also like to sell it as a Portable Document Format (PDF) e-book direct from a blog / web site that I will also use to market the book.

The Blog and Website

Below, you can see a screenshot of the blog that I set up originally to market and sell the second edition of "The Chrome Book".

It's beyond the scope of this book to get into the nitty-gritty of how to create a blog, and my intention here is merely to indicate that you can do so at www.blogger.com (log in with your Google account) using your chromebook; no PC required.

I designed the blog in such a way that it looked rather like a regular website with various "pages" of information in addition to the usual rolling commentary. But it wasn't a proper web site because of the pesky web address **http://thechromebook.blogspot.com** that marked it out as being a "blog". It is possible to associate a proper domain name with the blog using either the Google facility to purchase a domain name or by using a third party web domain manager such as GoDaddy (my preference) at www.godaddy.com. Once again, this is all entirely web-based, and in fact I chose a slightly different third option of registering my overarching company domain (**www.lotontech.com**) with GoDaddy and then *forwarding* the sub-domain **chromebook.lotontech.com** to the Blogger blog as shown here:

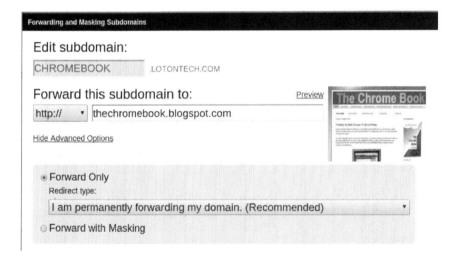

The PayPal Button

If you look back at the book's sales page on the blog, you will see that there is a link to purchase the **PDF e-book**. Clicking this link is equivalent to clicking a PayPal button that leads to the following payment page.

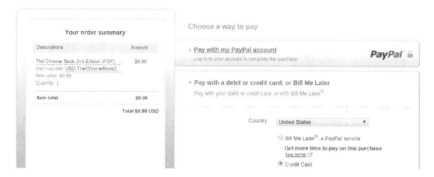

Note that my intention here is not to show you exactly how you can set yourself up to take PayPal payments, but to reassure you that you can do so using only web tools: in this case the PayPal web site at www.paypal.com.

Doing the Accounts

Once you start selling products like books and e-books, you need to maintain a set of accounts that record your incomings and outgoings to be reported to the tax authorities. I used to use a Windows PC software package called "Sage" to manage my company accounts, but now I use the fully web-based "Quickbooks Online" accounting package that can be found at http://quickbooksonline.intuit.com. Again, no PC required.

Chapter Summary

Ostensibly, the aim of this case study chapter has not been to present you with a blow-by-blow account of exactly how to publish a book, how to set up a web site and blog, how to take online payments, and how to manage your business (or personal) accounts. The real aim has been somewhat more subtle: to demonstrate that all of these things are possible by utilizing web apps and other websites via your chromebook... no PC required. It simply requires a different way of thinking from what you may have been used to.

And now for an admission: at the very last minute, I did resort to Microsoft Word to put a few "finishing touches" to the book such as adding the index into the print edition. I did this simply because I could, and not because I had to.

Find more **chromebook resources** including **books**, **chromebook computers** (if you don't already have one) and **compatible printers** at usa.thechromebook.info or uk.thechromebook.info.

12 - Soup Up your Chromebook with Crouton

Warning! This chapter is for advanced users only.

The Chrome OS operating system serves pretty much all the needs that we "cloud computing converts" might have, albeit via some roundabout routes at times. But since the Chrome OS sits atop the Linux operating system core, many of the more advanced chromebook users may speculate about whether their chromebooks can actually run the full-scale Linux operating system as an alternative to (or as well as) the Chrome OS... thereby providing access to some native programs – such as Skype – that are not currently supported on the browser-based Chrome OS. This question was particularly pressing for those early adopters who shelled out more than $1000 for a top-of-the-range Chromebook Pixel only to discover that it was basically web browser; albeit a very nice one.

The answer to the Linux question is "yes". There are several ways to achieve the feat of running Linux on a chromebook, but the most effective and flexible way appears to be by using a utility program called Crouton. So this will be our focus here.

Before we look at *souping up a chromebook with crouton* (get the joke?) I'd just like to set the record straight: as a cloud computing convert, I'm actually not all that interested in running full blown Linux on my chromebook, because it strikes me as contrary to the cloud computing ethos and the original raison d'etre for the chromebook. With that off my chest, let's take a look anyway.

Linux with Crouton—Step by Step

Note that the sequence of steps may differ slightly for different models of chromebook, and that some chromebook models may require you to throw a physical switch in order to enable the developer mode. For the record, these steps were performed on a Chromebook Pixel.

Note also that enabling the developer mode in the first step will cause the chromebook's local storage to be wiped, but this need not be a problem because all of your important data files should be stored safely on your Google Drive. It's best to double-check first, though.

Step #1: Enable Developer Mode

1. Shutdown your machine.
2. Press and hold **esc + refresh** while pushing the **power** button to switch on your computer.
3. Press **ctrl + d** to be prompted to enable developer mode, followed by **enter**.
4. The machine will take some time to reboot, but you can speed up the reboot by pressing **ctrl + d** again.

Step #2: Install Crouton

1. Download crouton from http://goo.gl/fd3zc.
2. Press **ctrl + alt + t** to launch a terminal window and type **shell** followed by the **enter** key.
3. Now type **sudo sh -e ~/Downloads/crouton -t xfce,touch** (followed by **enter**) to install Crouton.
4. Follow any prompts during the installation, and then finally...
5. Type Done! Start up an XFCE session with **sudo startxfce4** to start a Linux XFCE desktop session.

Unlike in an operating system dual-boot scenario, Crouton allows you to switch freely between the Linux and Chrome OS desktops using the following key combinations:

- On ARM processor chromebooks (e.g. Samsung) use the **ctrl + alt + shift + back** and **ctrl + alt + shift + forward** key combinations.
- On Intel processor chromebooks (e.g. Acer or Chromebook Pixel) use the **ctrl + alt + back** and **ctrl + alt + forward** (followed by **ctrl + alt + refresh**) key combinations.

The Result

The following picture shows the Linux desktop on my Chromebook Pixel after I made some changes to increase the screen font size etc. in the Linux display settings; without which the text would be microscopically small on my Chromebook Pixel's super hi-res screen):

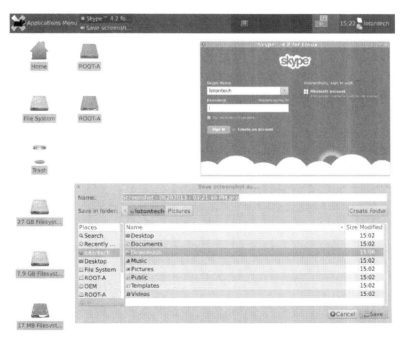

Note how on this Linux desktop I am running Skype, which at the time of writing cannot otherwise be run on a chromebook. Also notice the file manager window via which I am saving the captured screenshot into the Linux file system's **Downloads** folder; thereby allowing me to demonstrate that this is the very same Downloads folder as the one presented by the Chrome OS as shown here:

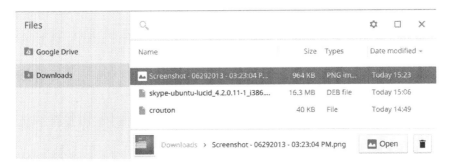

Getting Back to Normal

If, like me, you're actually not that keen on using the chromebook's developer mode in order to run Linux alongside the Chrome OS, you will be pleased to know that you can get "back to normal" simply by rebooting your chromebook and pressing the **Space** bar followed by **Enter** on the boot screen to disable the developer mode. All local data will be wiped, and your chromebook will return to normal.

The ChrUbuntu Alternative

While Crouton offers the most flexible way of running Linux in addition to the Chrome OS on a chromebook, it's not the only way. For those advanced users who prefer a more traditional "dual boot" scenario in which you choose your operating system at startup, there is an alternative tool called ChrUbuntu. Google it if you're interested.

Summary

As I have no doubt made clear, running Linux alongside the Chrome OS doesn't particularly interest me, especially since the Chrome OS itself is becoming more capable over time. But for the sake of completeness, it was only fair that I highlighted this possibility for those of you who may be interested.

Find more **chromebook resources** including **books, chromebook computers** (if you don't already have one) and **compatible printers** at usa.thechromebook.info or uk.thechromebook.info.

13 - My (and Your) Head in the Clouds

I do hope you're not superstitious, since we're finishing up with chapter 13!

You probably found that, like me, you were already spending 90% of your computing time on the web without even realizing it: reading and responding to emails, reading the news, and doing your online banking. You didn't need an over-engineered and virus-prone PC plus expensive software to do those things.

It may be true that you really do need to run some Windows PC software from time to time, but it doesn't mean you have to carry a PC around with you... especially if it's a desktop! Leave it at home or in the office, and connect to it remotely using the Chrome Remote Desktop app. It should work from any chromebook model; but on the supersize screen of the Chromebook Pixel I have found it to be just like sitting right in front of the PC screen. Otherwise, you might think about meeting your non-cloud-computing needs by *souping up your chromebook with Crouton* (Linux). But if you can wait long enough, you might not need to, because – ironically – the chromebook is becoming less cloud-dependent all the time; just look at the brand new QuickOffice integration.

The previous comment notwithstanding, I have made it clear throughout that I actually like the idea of going 100% cloud. What finally prompted me to aim towards full time residence in the cloud was the fact that, a couple of years ago, the screen on my Windows laptop computer flickered and died thereby rendering it my new 'desktop' computer with an external TV screen plugged in. It wasn't much use to me on the road, and in the time taken to consider a repair or replacement I became ever-more-reliant on whichever of my family's or friends' computers or other web connected devices came to hand. However and wherever I logged in, I had almost instantaneous access to the important documents I was working on via Google Docs (now Google Drive). There was no need to worry about a catastrophic hard disk crash or whether I had remembered to back up my data yesterday.

Fast forward to 2013, and here I am now sitting on my bed writing these very words in a Google Document via my Chromebook Pixel (but it could be any other chromebook). With one tap of the chromebook "switch windows" key I'm checking my Gmail in the Chrome browser, and in a separate browser tab I'm updating an entry in my Google Calendar. Meanwhile I'm listening to a song which the chromebook's built-in Audio Player found on my plugged-in USB stick and which it is playing in the background.

In previous editions of this book I summarized how I had transitioned almost entirely to cloud computing, but not entirely. The fact was that there were some things I needed to do in my personal and business lives that were simply not possible without a Windows PC. However, in the course of writing the previous chapter's case study chapter, I discovered that I could now do almost everything (or perhaps everything) that I needed to do using nothing but my chromebook. And I had every incentive to do so, literally, because of the whopping £1049 "investment" I had made in the top-of-the-range 2013 Chromebook Pixel compared with my more modest previous investment of £229 in the October 2012-vintage Samsung Chromebook. After committing to such an investment I wanted to make this cloud computing thing work for me... and I did.

The question is—will you?

But before we conclude, it's only fair for me to remind you that...

Google is Not the Only Cloud

In this book I have focused on cloud computing with Google hardware, software and services. I have assumed, or at least suggested, that you will adopt the set of cloud computing solutions offered by Google: Gmail for your email, Google Docs (via Google Drive) as your office application suite, and so on. But Google is not the only cloud computing show in town.

Those of you with a Microsoft Live ID or Hotmail email address can create and store Microsoft Word, PowerPoint, and Excel documents on your SkyDrive at http://skydrive.live.com. You might have so much investment in Microsoft Hotmail as your email provider that you're not quite ready to switch to Gmail just yet.

The good news is that the Chrome browser is simply a web browser, so – even when running on a chromebook computer – it should allow you to use alternative cloud solutions as well as (or instead of) those provided by Google. Indeed, Google is more open than some providers to the prospect of you using the best third-party solutions for your needs, else why would they provide a Chrome Web Store populated with third-party solutions?

Having painted this rosy picture of every vendor coexisting in the cloud in peace and harmony, I should warn you that you will need to double-check that your alternative cloud computing suite really will run on your chromebook + Chrome combo. Some Microsoft web sites may require or at least encourage you to install their Windows-dependent Silverlight browser extension.

Even if your alternative cloud computing suites run faultlessly, you may need to think about how the various cloud computing solutions fit together:

- Want to reroute your incoming email messages from Hotmail or Yahoo! Mail to your Gmail Inbox, or reroute your incoming Gmail to one of the other providers? No problem at all.
- Want to write a document initially using Google Docs, and then download it in Microsoft Word (.docx) format for uploading to your Windows SkyDrive for further editing? No Problem.
- Want to go the other way, and export a document created with the Microsoft Word Web App in a format other than the default **.docx** format? Well, it may not be so easy because the Microsoft Office Web Apps are designed to be an adjunct to the fully paid-up Microsoft Office Suite—so they assume that you have Word installed locally on your PC even though you are using the web-based alternative.

In a nutshell, interoperability between cloud computing solutions should be possible, and as my case study showed: with a little ingenuity and lateral thinking...it is. But, I have found that I can save myself a great deal of time and effort by wherever possible making Google my 'one stop shop' for cloud computing solutions.

When it comes to accessing my Google cloud, I don't have to do so from a Google device such as a chromebook or chromebox, even though I prefer to do so. I can access my Gmail and Google Docs from an Android mobile phone or Nexus tablet (okay, these are Google devices) or from a traditional Windows PC running the Chrome browser.

The choices are yours to make; but when all is said and done, for me, it's Google all the way.

For what is to come...

This third edition of "The Chrome Book" was written to coincide with the introduction of the Chromebook Pixel that was launched (from what I remember) with a tagline along the lines "For what is to come..."

One of the things to come just in time for this fourth edition was a version of the QuickOffice suite that runs on the Chromebook Pixel and ultimately on all chromebooks. I feel that this is still really only the beginning.

C H Rome

In the unlikely event that you haven't figured out the reasoning behind the pseudonym, let me spell it out for you... literally. It's **CHRome**.

Appendix – Google Play

Unlike the Amazon Kindle, the Apple iPad, and even the Microsoft Surface (RT version), which we may regard primarily as media-playing devices, Google chromebooks are not – to my knowledge – aimed specifically at consumers of books, movies, music and other media. This is why I have relegated my coverage of the Google Play media store to this appendix.

But first, an apology...for just referring to Google Play as a media store when in fact it also acts as the storefront for Google devices (like the Chromebook Pixel, Nexus phones and Nexus tablets) and Android apps (for your Android phone). Nevertheless, I regard Google Play as predominantly a media store—else why the name "Google **Play**"?

In your chromebook's app tray you should find three icons: one each for Google Play Music, Google Play Movies, and Google Play Books.

Play Music

Besides clicking on the app icon, you can also visit Google Play Music at **play.google.com/music**. It acts as your music manager in the cloud, to which you can upload songs from your existing collection (using a Windows PC or Mac, not your chromebook) or shop for songs in the online music store.

In the store you can purchase or preview individual songs or whole albums. Sometimes I like to click the **Play all** button for a particular album, which is a nice "free" way of listening to a set of excerpts from my favorite artists.

Play Books

Besides clicking on the app icon, you can also visit Google Play Books at **play.google.com/books**. As Google's equivalent of Amazon's Kindle book service, this acts as your book collection in the cloud.

You can of course read the books you have already purchased, as well as sampling and purchasing new books. Here's one that caught my eye:

Play Movies

Besides clicking on the app icon, you can also visit Google Play Movies at **play.google.com/movies**.

You should know what I'm going to say by now: Google Play Movies allows you to buy or rent movies to watch on your Chromebook.

Please Support Us!

If you enjoyed this book and found it useful, please support our publishing efforts by posting a positive review at Amazon.com, Amazon.co.uk or at your local Amazon. Thank you!

www.thechromebook.info

Index

Made in the USA
Lexington, KY
13 April 2014